HARVARD GERMANIC STUDIES I

Published under the direction of the
Department of Germanic Languages and Literatures

NOVALIS: THE VEIL OF IMAGERY

A Study of the Poetic Works of Friedrich von Hardenberg (1772–1801)

NOVALIS:
THE VEIL OF IMAGERY

A Study of the Poetic Works
of Friedrich von Hardenberg
(1772–1801)

BY

BRUCE HAYWOOD

MOUTON & CO
'S-GRAVENHAGE
1959

Printed in The Netherlands by Mouton & Co, Printers, The Hague

Library of Congress Catalog Card Number 59-7644

PREFACE

With this volume the Department of Germanic Languages and Literatures of Harvard University introduces a new series, the Harvard Germanic Studies. Our series is open to scholarly studies of high quality dealing with any aspect, literary or philological, of Germanic studies. A second volume is scheduled to appear soon, and we hope that many more will follow.

The generosity of members of the Visiting Committee of the Harvard Board of Overseers, which is concerned with this Department and the Busch-Reisinger Museum, has made this series financially possible. We are grateful to them, and to the Harvard University Press and Mouton and Company for their cooperation in helping to plan and launch this venture.

STUART ATKINS
BERNHARD BLUME
HENRY HATFIELD
TAYLOR STARCK

Cambridge, Massachusetts

ACKNOWLEDGMENTS

I wish to acknowledge my obligation to the many scholars and critics whose studies have aided me in the writing of this book. The most important of these I have listed in the appended bibliography. My thanks are also due to my former teachers and colleagues for their generous assistance and advice. I am particularly indebted to Professors Stuart Atkins and Henry Hatfield of Harvard University for their invaluable criticisms and suggestions. And to my family and friends who have aided and encouraged me I express my heartfelt gratitude.

B.H.

Kenyon College, March 1958

CONTENTS

INTRODUCTION

The reputation of Friedrich von Hardenberg, better known under his pen name Novalis, is today more secure than ever in his native Germany. The modern generation of German poets finds inspiration in his work, as did countless writers in the past. Novalis, together with his contemporaries Goethe and Hölderlin, remains one of the most vital influences in German literature. In the light of his unquestioned importance within the German tradition, his relative neglect in the English-speaking world is somewhat surprising. Novalis has never enjoyed the acclaim that the "cosmopolitan" Heinrich Heine, for example, has been accorded in England and North America. A variety of possible explanations for this apparent lack of response suggest themselves: Novalis' poetry is often obscure or ambiguous; his language presents more difficulties to the non-German than does that of most German writers; his work is limited in quantity; his intensely personal mode of expression does not readily lend itself to translation. Any one of these reasons might of itself limit the reputation of the poet, just as the Catholicizing tone of some of his writings might prejudice his acceptance. A more likely explanation for the neglect of Novalis, whose writings typify the German Romantic spirit to an unmatched degree, is to be found in the fact that Romanticism has not been the continuously vital force in the Anglo-American tradition that it has been in Germany since the eighteenth century. In the English-speaking world, where Goethe and Schiller, Classicists to most Germans, are considered Romantics, the poetry of Novalis must be judged ultra-Romantic and ultra-irrational. Certainly Novalis is the German Romantic poet *par excellence*, the pioneer of Romantic techniques in the lyric and the novel, the creator of that central symbol of the movement, the blue flower. In him is epitomized much that is usually associated with Romanticism in Germany: the subjective personifying of nature; the demand for the absolute; the crisis of religious experience; the yearning for the harmony of the Middle Ages; the concept of spiritual rebirth. It was from his works, more than from the critical writings of the Schlegels, that the younger Romantic poets took their inspiration. Novalis, to be sure, embodies in his poetry to a remarkable degree the ideas of the Schlegels—not, however, because he consciously appropriated these ideas, but because they were natural to him. He sensed intuitively the formless and naive poetry of the universe, that poetic spirit of which Friedrich Schlegel spoke in his *Gespräch über die Poesie* and which the Romantics took as their great subject. For Novalis, the poetic in the world was the only genuine reality, even as the poetic spirit in man was the proof of man's divine origin. All of his poetry is concerned ultimately with revealing and celebrating the poetic spirit. The Romantic movement in Germany found in Novalis its first lyric voice, a voice that has lost none of its freshness or persuasive quality.

Romantic as is the basic character of Novalis, he must be associated also with the strong mystic tradition in German literature. The Christian mystics of the Middle Ages and Jacob Böhme are his precursors, while with Hölderlin he shared the yearning for union with the first cause. Such modern mystics as Maeterlinck and Hermann Hesse reveal their kinship with Novalis in both theme and mode of expression. It is to Novalis the Romantic lyricist, however, that German literature is most indebted. With him begins that tendency, so marked in the German lyric, to seek in poetry what Novalis himself characterized as an indirect effect, like that of music. No poet before him had so imbued his creations with the music of words or so infused them with color. It is his bold experimentation with the expressive powers of language that, as much as his subject matter, has drawn later poets to his work.

The timeless quality of Novalis' poetry is perhaps nowhere more apparent than in its influence upon the giants of recent German literature. Rilke and Hofmannsthal, among the lyric poets, Hesse and Thomas Mann, among the novelists, are bound to Novalis with strong sympathetic ties. Motifs from Novalis are so often encountered in their writings as to suggest conscious borrowing. Mann's identification, for example, of life and art as hostile forces is owed primarily to Novalis, as is his association of genius with disease. Indeed, Mann's habitual mode of thinking in antitheses is strongly reminiscent of the Romantics and of Novalis in particular. It is Novalis' manner, however, of seeing all about him as symbol that identifies him most closely with poets of our time. Indeed, those later German poets whose work is concerned with universal symbols, rather than focused upon man in the manner of classical literature, are to a degree the spiritual heirs of Novalis.

The continuing influence of Novalis is the more remarkable when we survey the limited quantity of his poetic productions. He produced relatively little that can be correctly described as literature, a fact to be accounted for only in part by his death in his twenty-ninth year. For several years of his adult life Novalis displayed only an occasional interest in poetic creation, devoting himself to the study of philosophy, the sciences, and a variety of topics that occupied his attention from time to time. Not until three years before his death did he make a decisive turn back to poetry. Thus only two of his works were given final form, the *Hymnen an die Nacht* and the *Geistliche Lieder*, while he completed but a few chapters of his two symbolic novels, *Die Lehrlinge zu Sais* and *Heinrich von Ofterdingen*. The greater part of his writings consists of nonpoetic productions, an essay, "Die Christenheit oder Europa," and numerous aphorisms and fragmentary discourses on a diversity of topics.

In the past, much criticism of Novalis has suffered from too extensive a preoccupation with these nonpoetic productions and with autobiographical elements in his poetry. Such preoccupation is understandable. It is difficult to resist the brilliance of the far-ranging intellect revealed to us in the aphorisms and fragments. The poet's tragic love and early death make him, moreover, an appealingly dramatic figure. Nevertheless, the tendency of interpreters of Novalis' works to rely heavily on external elements has all too often marred their studies of the poet. The present study evolves in part from the conviction that interpretation without reference to external elements is not only possible but indeed desirable, and from the belief that, more than by any other critical method, the frequently veiled meaning of Novalis' works can be revealed by a study of their imagery.

CHAPTER I

THE NATURE AND FUNCTION
OF NOVALIS' IMAGERY

The purpose of any critical study of literature, C. Day Lewis has said in *The Poetic Image*, is that "of easing or widening or deepening" the response of the reader to the poetic work. A study of the imagery in the works of a particular poet must not depart from this principle. Imagery, whatever its importance in literature, is but one element of the total presentation, and the whole must not be forgotten in the study of the parts. Nevertheless, a study of the various elements that make up a literary work, such as imagery and metrical pattern, can often fulfill the demands of literary criticism as formulated by Lewis. While the part played in the total presentation by these elements may not be immediately apparent to the reader, they must inevitably modify and qualify his attitude towards the work. Imagery has been called the life-principle of poetry, and no justification for its study in poetry is needed. We must, however, guard against the dangers of making such a study the basis for conclusions as to personal traits of the author, his likes and dislikes, or his knowledge and lack of knowledge of specific things. Instead, an analysis of imagery should seek to give deeper insight into the poetic work itself and, where possible, shed new light on its meaning and aesthetic qualities. The recent study of Shakespeare's imagery by Wolfgang Clemen exemplifies such an approach to the question of the function of the poetic image. Professor Clemen's analysis, in *The Development of Shakespeare's Imagery,* reveals how imagery gradually becomes a language within language in Shakespeare's dramas, a subtle and indirect form of communication with his audience— "the favorite mode of expression of the later Shakespeare." It is the thesis of this study of Novalis' poetry that for the German poet, too, imagery served as such a language within language and method of indirect communication; indeed, that imagery was regarded by Novalis as the prime mode of poetic expression.

The poetic image may be defined as any evocation through words of a sensuous object, though such an image may again be described as either "literal" or "figurative." The literal image is a figure of contiguity, suggesting a relationship logically or quantitatively analyzable, as, for example, the image of winter in Shakespeare's "When icicles hang by the wall/And Dick the shepherd blows his nail." The rhetorical figures metonomy (cause for effect, container for contained, etc.) and synecdoche (part for whole, matter for use, etc.) may also be cited as examples of literal images, since again the relationships involved are readily discernible. The figurative image, on the other hand, is one of similarity, the principle of such tropes of poetry as metaphor and simile, personification and catachresis, as it depicts one thing in terms usually denoting another with which it may be regarded by the poet as analogous. Thus, figurative images are employed by Blake in his "Auguries of Innocence" when he writes, "To see a World in a Grain of Sand/And a Heaven in a Wild Flower. . . ." The poetic image may further become a symbol if it recurs persistently in the work, with a function of linking two or more areas of reference, or if it refers to another object but demands attention in its own right. The image of the blue flower in Novalis' *Heinrich von Ofterdingen*, for example, may be described as a symbol by either definition. There is danger in venturing beyond such basic definitions, for in our concern to classify and categorize we may forget the real purpose of the study of imagery.

Both literal and figurative imagery is to be found in profusion in the works of Novalis, and this imagery, as I have suggested, is of great importance in his poetry, a vital part of the total presentation. Imagery cannot, of course, be studied in isolation from its context if the study is to be a meaningful contribution to the appreciation of the poetic work. What the value of any poetic image is can only be determined from an examination of its function in its context. A statistical study of imagery will tell us little about the poetry in which the images have their being. The isolation of the image from its context may rob it of much of its value, particularly when it is a part of an image pattern and draws its full meaning from its relationship to other images in the work. The imagery is, in fact, best integrated with the poetic work and best contributes to the totality of the presentation when the images form a pattern and the imagery is congruous to the theme of the work. Such congruity is realized in the mature poetry of Novalis, and it will be shown in the various chapters of this study that a pattern of imagery is discernible in both his verse and prose works, a pattern that reveals the poet's meanings and attitudes more clearly than do his explicit statements.

Novalis' use of imagery as his prime mode of expression was determined, it would seem, by a variety of factors which may be usefully examined before turning to a study of the imagery in the works themselves. In his fragments and aphorisms Novalis set down his ideas and views on the variety of topics that occupied his attention.[1] Whether because of his early death, the Romantic cultivation of the fragment, or simply an inability to complete projects undertaken, few of these ideas were ever completely developed. In order to obtain a rounded picture of the poet's views on any subject we must thus depend on cross reference and the expansion and analysis of isolated statements. This is particularly true of his theories of the nature and function of the poetic image, for Novalis showed relatively little concern for the theories and problems of literature until the decisive turn to poetry, late in his short life. His communications to his friends, too, are less concerned with theory than with his plans and projects. In view of this we could scarcely expect to find any developed theory of imagery. Yet there is sufficient evidence in his writings to show both that Novalis speculated on the nature of the poetic image and that he came to recognize distinct functions of imagery in his own poetry.

Neither Novalis' letters nor his diaries contain any mention of poetic imagery, nor do we have any indication that he discussed the topic with his closest friends, Ludwig Tieck and the Schlegel brothers. Even his own notes are relatively bare of allusions to this subject. In an aphorism in "Blütenstaub," however, we find him early expressing a felt need for metaphorical language—"How often one feels the poverty of words, when one seeks to express

---

[1] Citations from Novalis in my text are to the *Schriften*, ed. Paul Kluckhohn (Leipzig, 1929), I-IV. The translations of the citations are in every case my own.

exactly several ideas at one fell swoop" ("Wie oft fühlt man die
Armut an Worten, um mehre Ideen mit einem Schlage zu tref-
fen" [II, 26])—and references to imagery do become more frequent in his writings as his interest focused on poetry. (The terms
employed by Novalis, for which in this study the more general term
"image" is frequently substituted, are "Trope," "Bild," "Metapher,"
"Gleichnis," "Sinnbild," and "Symbol.") There is evidence, for
example, that Novalis observed the practices of other authors:
"Similes à la Lessing, from *everyday life*" ("Gleichnisse à la Lessing,
aus dem gemeinen Leben" [III, 331]), and that he experimented with image making: "Images—allegoric images taken from
nature. My recent one of the fountain. Rainbows about the
fountain-head. Rising clouds as the fountain's prayers" ("Bilder—
allegorische aus der Natur. Mein neuliches vom Springbrunnen—
Regenbogen um die Quelle. Aufsteigende Wolken als Quellen-
gebete" [III, 291]). We find him, too, speculating on the "strange"
qualities of metaphor, that is, of traditional allegorism: "Strange
extension of a *metaphor*—e.g. love is sweet, thus to love are as-
cribed all the qualities of sugar" ("Seltsame Ausführung eines
Gleichnisses—z.B. die Liebe ist süss, also kommt ihr alles zu,
was dem Zucker zukommt" [III, 311]). However, these indications
of an active, theoretical interest in the problem are less significant
for Novalis' poetic productions than other, less explicit statements.

It becomes increasingly clear to the reader of Novalis' notes and
aphorisms that he was by nature disposed to the use of figurative
language. It is evident, too, that he regarded imagery as the uni-
quely poetic element in literature: "The poet borrows all his ma-
terials except his images" ("Alle Materialien borgt der Dichter,
bis auf die Bilder" [III, 14]). This belief, I would suggest, accounts
for the fact that the poets in his works are characterized by their
use of metaphorical language. Many poets seem to have found
in imagery a means to express the relationship between things, and
the relationship between things and feelings. We find Novalis on
one occasion commenting in typically aphoristic fashion on his
sensing of the sympathy between things, and between things and
himself: "Whatever we love we find everywhere, and everywhere
we see similarities. The greater our love, the broader and more
varied this world of similarities" ("Was man liebt, findet man
überall und sieht überall Ähnlichkeiten. Je grösser die Liebe, desto

weiter und mannigfaltiger diese ähnliche Welt" [II, 47]). Then, after reflection on the nature of the poetic image, he reached the conclusion that "the external elements of poetic language seem to be strange formulations of analogous relationships, symbolic representations of the *poetic* in phenomena" (". . . die Äusserlichkeiten der poetischen Rede scheinen sonderbare Formeln ähnlicher Verhältnisse, sinnbildliche Zeichen des Poetischen an den Erscheinungen zu sein" [III, 329]).

Perhaps even more conducive to the use of metaphor, however, is Novalis' view of life, a view like that expressed in Goethe's "All that is transitory is merely a symbol . . . ." Such a view may naturally lead to the representation of life in metaphorical terms. Man, his existence, and the world about him were for Novalis symbolic, a view which, to be sure, is common to all idealistic philosophy. Of particular interest to this study, however, and a fact which points to one function of imagery for Novalis is that he invariably expressed this idea of the symbolic nature of existence in terms taken from formal rhetoric: "What is man? A perfect trope of the spirit" ("Was ist der Mensch? Ein vollkommner Trope des Geistes" [II, 352]). "The world is a universal trope of the spirit, a symbolic representation of it" ("Die Welt ist ein Universaltropus des Geistes, ein symbolisches Bild desselben" [II, 384]). Nowhere is this viewpoint embodied more succinctly than in the pointed equation, "Man: metaphor" ("Der Mensch: Metapher" [II, 350]). History, too, was viewed metaphorically by the poet, as will be demonstrated in our discussion of the *Hymnen an die Nacht* and *Heinrich von Ofterdingen*. This fact is also exemplified in the essay, "Die Christenheit oder Europa," the poet's visionary appeal for a revival of the medieval European union. There Novalis invites his readers, in order that they may understand history's pattern, to apply to history the "magic wand of analogy": "I refer you to history. Seek similar moments in history's instructive concatenation and learn to use the magic wand of analogy" ("An die Geschichte verweise ich euch, forscht in ihrem belehrenden Zusammenhang nach ähnlichen Zeitpunkten, und lernt den Zauberstab der Analogie gebrauchen" [II, 78]). When we find Novalis confessing, "Everywhere we seek the infinite [or the absolute] and always we find only the finite" ("Wir suchen überall das Unbedingte, und finden immer nur Dinge" [II, 15]), the juxta-

position of "Unbedingte" and "Dinge" suggests at once that his
way to the absolute will be through "Dinge," through imagery.
This assumption is supported by Novalis' own statements that all
knowledge is the result of association and analogy—"All cognition,
knowledge, etc. can be traced back to comparison and correspondence" ("Auf Vergleichen, Gleichen lässt sich wohl alles Erkennen, Wissen etc. zurückführen" [II, 335])—and that we understand most clearly that which is concretely depicted: "We understand a thing most easily when we see it in representation . . . (God
Himself is comprehensible only through representation)" ("Man
versteht eine Sache am leichtesten, wenn man sie repräsentiert
sieht . . . (Gott selbst ist nur durch Repräsentation verständlich)"
[III, 66]). Indeed, Novalis' "magic idealism," which has been the
subject of much discussion, is essentially nothing more than metaphorical representation—the representation of the abstract in terms
of the concrete, and the seeing of the physical as a manifestation
of the spiritual: "If you are unable to make your thoughts perceptible indirectly (and by chance), do the opposite and make external
phenomena perceptible directly (and arbitrarily)—which is tantamount to saying that if you cannot make your thoughts into external
phenomena, make external phenomena into thoughts. If you cannot create from a thought an independent spirit (detached from
you *and now foreign to you*—that is, existing as an external
phenomenon), do the opposite with external phenomena—translate these into thoughts. Both processes are idealistic. He who
has complete control over both processes is the *magic idealist*"
("Wenn ihr die Gedanken nicht mittelbar (und zufällig) vernehmbar machen könnt, so macht doch umgekehrt die äussern Dinge
unmittelbar (und willkürlich) vernehmbar—welches ebensoviel ist
als: wenn ihr die Gedanken nicht zu äussern Dingen machen
könnt, so macht die äussern Dinge zu Gedanken. Könnt ihr einen
Gedanken nicht zur selbständigen, sich von euch absondernden—
und nun euch fremd—das heisst äusserlich vorkommenden
Seele machen, so verfahrt umgekehrt mit den äusserlichen Dingen—
und verwandelt sie in Gedanken. Beide Operationen sind ideali-
stisch. Wer sie beide vollkommen in seiner Gewalt hat, ist der
magische Idealist" [III, 110]).
  While it is not the primary purpose of this study to examine
Novalis' philosophy, it would seem that his preoccupation with idea-

listic philosophy led him to important conclusions as to the function of imagery in poetry. His aphorisms on the metaphorical nature of life antedate his study of poetic imagery, and he seems to have been drawn to the view that since life itself was metaphorical, metaphor must be the poet's way of depicting life. In one of his later aphorisms Novalis said, "Everything is a fairy tale" ("Alles ist ein Märchen" [III, 220]), and as this study will later demonstrate "metaphorical" might well be substituted here for "a tale," while still later this concept was to become the principle, "The tale is, so to speak, the *canon of poetry*—all poetry must have fairy tale qualities" ("Das Märchen ist gleichsam der Kanon der Poesie—alles Poetische muss märchenhaft sein" [III, 248]). Novalis' aim as a poet would appear to have been to produce what he called "transcendental poetry": "Transcendental poetry is a mixture of philosophy and poesy. Basically it embraces every transcendental function and, indeed, the transcendental itself" ("Die transzendentale Poesie ist aus Philosophie und Poesie gemischt. Im Grunde befasst sie alle transzendentale Funktionen und enthält in der Tat das Transzendentale überhaupt" [II, 327]). In this kind of poetry imagery would have the function of linking earthly existence to the transcendental and, at the same time, of depicting the symbolic nature of the transcendental world: "Through the practice of transcendental poetry we may expect to create a system of tropes that apprehends the laws of the symbolic structure of the transcendental world" ("Von der Bearbeitung der transzendentalen Poesie lässt sich eine Tropik erwarten—die die Gesetze der symbolischen Konstruktion der transzendentalen Welt begreift" [II, 327]). This symbolic representation of the relationship between the concrete and the abstract, between the immanent and the transcendent, would appear to determine the nature of much of Novalis' imagery and to be one important function of his metaphor. Such a function is, indeed, readily discernible in the poet's works, and in this respect he is a part of a tradition that goes back to the personification images of ancient myth. There is, however, another, more personal function of Novalis' imagery, to which he refers explicitly at only one point in his writings. Yet this function, I believe, is of prime importance in his works. In the preface to one of his collections of aphorisms, "Glauben und Liebe," Novalis speaks of a special language of imagery, a secret mode of communication with a select few: "If you wish to communicate some secret to just a few people in a large, mixed company and you are not sitting next to them, you have to speak a special language. This special language can be a foreign language in terms either of its *sounds* or of its *images*. The latter will be a language of tropes and enigmas" ("Wenn man mit wenigen, in einer grossen, gemischten Gesellschaft etwas Heimliches reden will und man sitzt nicht nebeneinander, so muss man in einer besondern Sprache reden. Diese besondre Sprache kann entweder eine dem Ton nach oder den Bildern nach fremde Sprache sein. Dies letztere wird eine Tropen- und Rätselsprache sein" [II, 47]). In this instance, then, imagery would serve a dual purpose. It would be an enigmatic language to the uninitiated, to the unpoetic for whom phantasy has no meaning, and would bar their access to the poet's secrets. At the same time, it would be a special language through which he might communicate to those few sympathetic to poetry and to himself. This idea of communication with the initiated alone is further developed, as Novalis continues in the preface, "Many people have thought that one ought to use a language of savants for delicate subjects that might be profaned, e.g. one ought to write in Latin on such subjects. It would seem more to the point to try to speak in ordinary, everyday language in such a way that the only one who could understand would be the one who was supposed to understand. Any real secret must automatically exclude the profane. Whoever understands it is automatically and justly an *initiate*" ("Viele haben gemeint, man solle von zarten, missbrauchbaren Gegenständen eine gelehrte Sprache führen, z.B. lateinisch von Dingen der Art schreiben. Es käme auf einen Versuch an, ob man nicht in der gewöhnlichen Landessprache so sprechen könnte, dass es nur der verstehn könnte, der es verstehn sollte. Jedes wahre Geheimnis muss die Profanen von selbst ausschliessen. Wer es versteht, ist von selbst, mit Recht, Eingeweihter").[2] Novalis' imagery is, I believe, the special language

[2] It is interesting to find Novalis' close friend Friedrich Schlegel making a similar reference to a special language within language. In "Über die Philosophie" he speaks of a "Sprache in der Sprache" when discussing the language of philosophers. While Schlegel makes no explicit mention of imagery, his conclusion is remarkably like that of Novalis: "For the best thing about this fine Sanskrit of a Hemsterhuis or a Plato is that only

by which he communicates his secrets to the "initiated," to those who share his belief in the metaphorical nature of life and in the power of poetry to reveal the transcendent through the immanent.

In an analysis of Novalis' works it becomes apparent that the poet's growing theoretical interest in imagery was accompanied by a development in the use of imagery in his poetry. His early poems are rich in imagery, though only on occasion is this imagery more than conventional ornament or extravagant hyperbole. Gradually this type of imagery is replaced almost entirely by imagery that is an integral part of the poetry and which relates more naturally to its context. Finally, in the major verse and prose works, imagery becomes the language within language to which we have referred. In these works is a pattern of imagery, often not immediately discernible, but which, as it is developed, subtly suggests the poet's attitudes and reveals the meaning of the work. It must again be emphasized, however, that the full value of the imagery is realized only in relation to its context. It cannot, therefore, be studied in isolation. In many instances a single image acquires greater significance, too, as it complements and is complemented by other images in the work. An image that is not a part of a pattern, however, may also serve to deepen our understanding of the passage in which it appears. Novalis invariably employs an image to express in palpable terms the abstract idea with which he is momentarily concerned. Such images are a vital part of the poet's language of imagery. We find also on occasion purely hyperbolic images that heighten expression for an instant but are then not developed. This type of image is found extensively in "Die Christenheit oder Europa." Most readers of Novalis will be familiar with his poignant metaphorical representation in that essay of the results of the rise of atheistic philosophy after the Reformation: "hatred of religion . . . transformed the infinite,

---

those understand it who are supposed to understand" ("Denn das ist das schönste an diesem schönen Sanskrit eines Hemsterhuis oder Plato, dass nur die es verstehn, die es verstehn sollen"). Friedrich Schlegel, *Seine Prosaische Jugendschriften,* ed. Jacob Minor, (Vienna, 1882), II, 335. Examination of the succinct account of the critical theories of the Schlegel brothers given by René Wellek, *A History of Modern Criticism* (New Haven, 1955), II, 5-73, reveals several similar instances of correspondence between the ideas of the Schlegels concerning the rôle of imagery in poetry and those of Novalis.

creative music of the universe into the uniform clattering of a monstrous mill, a mill driven by and floating upon the stream of chance, a self-sufficient mill without architect or miller and in fact a true *perpetuum mobile,* a mill that is crushing itself" ("der Religionshass . . . machte die unendliche schöpferische Musik des Weltalls zum einförmigen Klappern einer ungeheuren Mühle, die vom Strom des Zufalls getrieben und auf ihm schwimmend, eine Mühle an sich, ohne Baumeister und Müller und eigentlich ein echtes Perpetuum mobile, eine sich selbst mahlende Mühle sei" [II, 75]). In its context such imagery seems to have a function quite different from that of the imagery in the poetic works. It serves at a given moment to capture the imagination of the reader by its brilliance and emotional quality, and thus make him receptive to the author's views. (Clearly, in this case Novalis is not seeking to communicate with an initiated few, but rather to impress a broad audience with his appeal for a new united Europe.) As a result, the imagery does not seem to be an integral part of the work but lies, as it were, on the surface. Nevertheless, the frequency with which Novalis employs in the essay images of striking forcefulness and poetic quality is indicative of his propensity to use imagery as his prime mode of expression.

The nature of Novalis' imagery is determined to a considerable extent, as I have suggested, by his belief in the metaphorical character of the world and of life itself. Thus, his metaphor endows the physical world with spiritual qualities, represents the abstract through the concrete, and makes of the characters in his prose works symbols of universal human experience. In this respect his imagery is essentially like that of other poets who have sought to express such a philosophy through metaphor. We must beware of crediting it with unique or original qualities. In any case, it is virtually impossible to determine unequivocally the originality of a poet's imagery. We must also guard against seeing the preferred use of certain images as necessarily an indication of convictions shared with contemporaries or predecessors. "Anyone who writes constantly," John Dover Wilson[3] has said, "knows that a metaphor, perhaps picked up from another writer (as many of Shakespeare's were), and entirely unconnected with his own

---

[3] In his preface to Wolfgang Clemen's *The Development of Shakespeare's Imagery,* p. v.

interests, may grow upon him and become a habit of mind." We can at best establish whether, in his choice of imagery, the poet displays preference for certain figures and whether these images have particular areas of reference. Thus, in Novalis' works we can discern a gradual growth of preference for metaphor over simile, particularly for metaphor of animistic projection. There is ample evidence, too, of his preferred use of light and color images of considerable variety, of water imagery, and of metaphor of growth. Particularly striking is his erotic imagery, prominent in his early poetry as well as in his mature work. It is through these images to which he most often turns that Novalis seeks to break the bonds of conventional language, to express the inexpressible and make palpable the abstract by clothing it in metaphor. Much of this imagery has an esoteric quality. The poet boldly embodies in metaphor a relationship that cannot fail to strike the reader as unusual and indicative of Novalis' remarkable flair for analogy. Yet, when the context permits, Novalis willingly exploits traditional metaphor, invoking imagery from Biblical sources, the hymns of the Christian church, and from popular fairy tales. Once again, however, it should be pointed out that we must not draw from these practices illegitimate conclusions as to the significance to the poet of the *content* of these images. The only legitimate conclusions we may draw so far as Novalis the poet is concerned are that his thoughts seem naturally to have crystallized in poetic images, or at least that metaphor better expressed his thoughts than did abstract words, and that the image was the means by which he was best able to objectify his thoughts and feelings.

At this point we may refer to two marked stylistic characteristics of Novalis' poetry that are related in some measure to his use of imagery. The first is a remarkable fondness for periphrasis, the avoidance of direct identification that seems to be determined by Novalis' practice of viewing all about him metaphorically. To a degree this usage contributes to the symbolic character of his work, as when, for example, characters in his novels are made representative of universal human attributes through identification by title—"the apprentice," "the youth," "the teacher," "the old man"—rather than by name. The second characteristic derives from Novalis' love of epithet, a trait of the Romantic poets generally. In Novalis' poetry the adjective is often an important part of a greater image. Again, the use of an epithet first applied to some object to qualify a second, apparently unrelated object inevitably links the two together in the mind of the reader. Thus, the epithet is often of importance in a developing image pattern.

Nature and function of imagery are combined to a remarkable degree in Novalis' poetry. The prime function of his imagery would seem to be to reveal to those sympathetic to his views his interpretation of life. Accordingly his imagery displays the metaphorical nature of the poet's world. Again, when the poet reveals the nature of certain characters in his novels through their practice of expressing themselves in imagery, the nature of their imagery subtly conveys their inner qualities. Thus a use of literal imagery or simple metaphor suggests that individual's naïveté and intuitive powers. Novalis' poets, on the other hand, are characterized by the bold, imaginative nature of their metaphor.[4] The true quality of Novalis' imagery, I would suggest, lies in this equation of its nature and function and in the way his language of imagery is integrated with the totality of the presentation. As Novalis developed as an artist, imagery became the mode of expression to which he most readily turned, and it is through his imagery that we may best reach the heart of his work. It is most indicative of Novalis' belief that imagery was the peculiar language of the poet that the growth of the poetic spirit in the youthful hero of *Heinrich von Ofterdingen* is revealed through his increasing propensity to think and express himself in poetic images.

[4] The one exception is the poet Klingsohr in *Heinrich von Ofterdingen*, though for reasons that will be made plain in my analysis of that work.

CHAPTER II

NOVALIS' EARLY POETRY (1785-1797)

Early Experiments (1785-1794)

There is little evidence in Novalis' early poetry of the remark-able lyric powers that were to manifest themselves in the last years of his life. We find in his early productions scant indication of the talent that was to burst forth with such suddenness just before his death. Yet it would be wrong to give the impression that those works of his last years on which Novalis' reputation rests were his first serious attempts at creation. Between the years 1785 and 1794, that is from the age of thirteen until the completion of his university studies, Novalis wrote more than two hundred completed poems, though only one of these, "Klagen eines Jünglings" (I, 325ff), was published during his lifetime. In addition he planned many works of more ambitious scope—novels, dramas, and epic poems, which were never executed. These early productions are generally unknown—none of them, to my knowledge, has ever appeared in an anthology of verse—and they scarcely merit atten-tion, except in so far as they contribute to an understanding of the poet's development. Few critics have made more than passing reference to Novalis' early attempts at poetry. We have been almost invited to believe, indeed, that it was the experience of the death of his fiancée, Sophie von Kühn, that turned Novalis overnight into the poet who wrote the "Hymns to Night." Such misrepresen-tation of the facts, of course, serves the purposes of biographical dramatization. Yet, significant as the Sophie experience was for Novalis, by the time he fell in love with her he had already passed through the initial stages of his artistic development. Novalis' school and university years were a time of experiment and practice when he wrestled with the conventionalities of contemporary usage, to emerge eventually as an independent poet. The poems of those years are the products of an immature talent, written by

a young man who sought to master the intricate problems of form
by imitating the popular poetry of the day. In fact, any real development on the part of their author is not immediately apparent.

For his edition of Novalis' works, Paul Kluckhohn selected
some hundred of the better poems of this period, including all the
poems in the earlier editions of Minor and Heilborn. There would
be little value, as Kluckhohn points out in his introduction, in
publishing the remaining poems, since these have even less claim
to artistic merit.[1] For want of evidence that would enable us to
date the poems accurately, Kluckhohn has arranged them in loose
chronological order and in genre groupings, relying largely on the
evidence of the manuscripts—the author's practice of writing
several poems on one sheet of paper, the predominance of certain
thematic and stylistic characteristics, and orthographical evidence.
To draw conclusions as to the date of composition from such
evidence as the models imitated by Novalis or the poems which
reveal the influence of individual poets would be dangerous.
Novalis imitated more than one poet at a time and was fond of
experimenting with different genres. It would thus be misleading
to speak of an Anacreontic or an elegaic "period" in his early
poetry. Nor can we relate the poems to incidents or experiences
in the poet's life, for he frequently places himself in imagined
situations for the purpose of his theme, as is well illustrated by
poems on the death of his father and to his dying sister, written
when both were in good health. It is more rewarding to treat the
poems collectively as the first steps in Novalis' artistic development, as self-imposed exercises in poetic practice. It is obvious
that Novalis felt that the way to become a poet was by writing
poetry, and he chose to imitate the work of established poets.
Bürger, the "Hainbund" poets, Gotter, Schiller all served him as
models. Like most young poets, Novalis was most concerned with
problems of form. For example, four sonnets addressed to August
Wilhelm Schlegel (I, 283ff), while part of one context, display
skillful variation of rhyme scheme. However, Novalis' concern
for metrical pattern and rhyme frequently lead him to tasteless

---

[1] On the occasion of an auction of Novalis manuscripts in Berlin,
December 20, 1931, Richard Samuel published a descriptive catalog, the
quotations in which amply support Kluckhohn's claim to have published
the better poems of this period.

interpolation, as we can illustrate in the poem "An mein Schwert"
(I, 309f): "And strike the man who fights for slaves/(In truth,
he is a miserable wretch),/Guided by my hand" ("Und hau den,
der für Sklaven ficht/(Gewiss, er ist ein schlechter Wicht),/Ge-
fülht von meinei Hand"). The variety of forms used by Novalis
at this period is equalled only by the diversity of his themes. He
experimented with almost every genre of poetry then popular.
We find that a majority of the poems could be classified as
Anacreontic, although there are also odes to individuals, and
groups of elegaic, patriotic and didactic verses.

It is difficult for us to take Novalis' early poetry seriously.
Poetry seems at this stage to have meant little more for him than
a social grace or a common bond with men he respected—Bürger,
Jacobi, the Schlegels. Novalis is here poetaster rather than poet.
He is a *poseur*, lecturing in one poem on the need for a "philosophy of life" ("An Filidor" (I, 304), and elsewhere), while in
another praising the delights of love and wine. Yet again we must
emphasize that these poems are, in the main, experiments with
theme and form. Novalis can scarcely have placed any greater
value on them later in life than we do now. Certainly many of the
excesses and failings of these poems can be attributed to the
models from which they were copied. Novalis was an imitator
at this stage, and it is not to be expected that the copy will be
better than the original.

If Novalis is an imitator of theme and form, we must expect
that his imagery, too, will be influenced by contemporary practice.
Despite occasional bold imaginativeness, Novalis is generally dependent on his models both in choice and use of imagery. The
earliest of these poems, written when he was still a schoolboy, are
relatively free from imagery. What imagery we do find is confined
to elementary metaphor and simile—"Your life ought happily to
glide by/Like a serene summer's night" ("Ihr Leben müsste froh
verfliessen/Gleich einer heitern Sommernacht" [I, 273])—or to
rare, more ambitious use of personification and metonomy. From
this point on, however, we see an ever-increasing use of imagery
in Novalis' early poetry. This profusion of imagery cannot be
accounted for completely by a love of ornament and hyperbole.
For the most part, however, this imagery is not integrated, but
seems to have been added, like the Elizabethan conceit, almost as

afterthought. Most noticeable and most objectionable is Novalis'
use of classical reference. We meet all too frequently the names
Apollo, Euphrosyne, and Thalia, and the use of six such references in a poem of thirteen lines ("An Jacobi" [I, 293]) is a fairly
representative example. It is in the poems dedicated to his friends
and fellow poets that Novalis is at his worst, displaying too self-
consciously his familiarity with classical mythology. This often
goes beyond bad taste to sheer incongruity. In a fairly simple
Anacreontic poem one is horrified to come across "a leg/Apt to
unseal even Cato's virtue" ("ein Bein,/Geschickt selbst Katos
Tugend zu entsiegeln" [I, 302]). Again, a transition like that
from "rosebud mouth" and "Cupid's sweet games" to "Voltaire's
'Pucelle'" and "Phanias, cooled by the juice of grapes" is much
too abrupt for later taste. Most incongruous of all, however, is
the imagery of "An Laurens Eichhörnchen" (I, 294). Addressing
the squirrel that receives the caresses for which he longs, the poet
says: "O were luck to smile on me,/Grant me your form for just
one day,/Then no glance would suffice for me,/The fate of Leda
would be hers" ("O lächelte mir doch das Glück,/Liess einen Tag
mich in dich fahren,/Dann mich begnügte nicht ein Blick,/Sie
würde Ledas Los erfahren"). The grotesquely erotic note of these
lines is present in many of the early poems. It is clear that Novalis
found Anacreontic verse the easiest to copy. The imagery of his
Anacreontic poetry is again that of his models. The conventional,
trite imagery—"Rosenwangen," "Zephir," "Flor," and so on—is
repeated *ad nauseam*. There is the familiar love of allegorical
personification—"Goodness ... bewitcher of hearts," "Love ...
conqueror of all" (I, 282)—and the dancing shepherds and
maidens, whose names—Minchen, Molly, Laura—are all too
familiar. The "nature" which is invariably the background for
Novalis' lovers is a painted, stylized nature, always in bloom,
a theatrical backdrop: "About me dance flowery field and lea/
And every grass blade laughs,/And more blissfully does nature
bloom/Dressed in her spring array" ("Um mich tanzt Blumentrift
und Flur,/Und jedes Hälmchen lacht,/Und seliger blüht die
Natur/Mir in der Frühlingstracht" [I, 295]). At this stage Novalis
conveys no sense of the deep sympathy for nature so evident in
his later work. Nor does he develop the parallelism between
nature and man's emotions that forms the basis of much of his

later imagery. Characteristic of this period is the parallelism of "Die Erlen" (I, 299), where, conventionally enough, the growth of the alders symbolizes the growth of the lovers' passion. Once again Novalis is following the example of his contemporaries, though many of the poems have a certain lightness and musical quality that compensate to some degree for the conventional nature of their imagery and theme.

A marked characteristic of Novalis' early poetry is his practice of piling one image upon another. So intent is he on image-making that, rather than develop one image already created, he heaps a new one upon it. The poetry of these years thus has a peculiarly crowded aspect: "For yet her feeble arm is not skilled/Quickly to bend Apollo's bowstring,/And, like the silver swan, wing through the ether/To where Cythere's grove swims in odors sweet/And Thalia tunes gold for folksongs" ("Denn noch ist nicht ihr schlaffer Arm/Gewandt Apollos Sehne schnell zu biegen,/Und trotz dem Silberschwan den Äther zu durchfliegen,/Hin, wo Cytheres Hain in Wohlgerüchen schwimmt,/Und Thalia das Gold zu Volksgesängen stimmt" [I, 280]). It is a lack of critical judgment that permits him to follow simile by metaphor and again by simile: "... like one of the immortals the soul soars up/On the wings of the swan, in flight like a skater on ice" ("... wie der Unsterblichen eine die Seele sich aufschwingt/Mit den Flügeln des Schwans, im Schwung wie ein Läufer des Eises" [I, 311f]). This same lack of critical sense accounts for the frequently exaggerated nature of Novalis' metaphor. His image-making is often bold to the point that it is objectionable. Personifying the Harz mountains in a patriotic outburst, he goes on: "Generously you permitted that your bowels/Should be grubbed with busy hand/For ruinous gold and silver orc/By man's insatiable thirst" ("Gütig liessest du zu, dass dir dein Eingeweid/Mit der emsigen Hand durchwühlt/Nach verderbendem Gold und nach dem Silbererz/Unersättlicher Menschendurst" [I, 311f]). Such excess produces alarming incongruity and frequently results in poems that consist of one long, exaggerated hyperbole.

I have to this point emphasized the worst aspects of Novalis' choice and use of imagery in his early work. These criticisms are justified, however, and necessary if we are to obtain a true picture of his development. The examples quoted are all typical and

could be supported by numerous instances of the same type. The
poetry of Novalis' early period has little to recommend it and it
is apparent that Novalis has not succeeded, at this stage, in
breaking with the worst in contemporary practice so far as his
imagery is concerned. Whereas his mastery of technique in meter
and rhyme develops markedly in this early poetry—one finds
little artificial interpolation of verses to fill out a metrical pattern
in the later poems of this group—in his making and use of
imagery Novalis has made less progress. Yet some development
is apparent. On infrequent occasions one meets with an imaginative metaphor that stands apart from his conventional imagery.
One such example is to be found in "Die Liebe" (I, 296f). The
general imagery of the poem is conventional enough: "And round
about me wakens/The choir of nightingales/And every meadow
laughs..." ("Und rund um mich erwachet/Der Nachtigallen
Chor/Und jede Aue lachet..."), but the final verse of this
stanza, "And every shepherd is an ear" ("Und jeder Hirt ist
Ohr"), is striking in its freshness and directness. There is evidence,
too, of a growing ability to integrate the imagery of the poem with
its mood and theme. The poem "Die Kahnfahrt" (I, 320 f) is
clearly the work of a maturing poet and shows definite skill in
composition. Whereas in the poem already quoted, "Die Erlen"
(I, 299), the parallelism between the growth of the poet's love and
the growth of the alders is made all too explicit, in this poem the
parallelism between nature and the poet's thoughts (unremarkable
as these are) is subtly expressed through the imagery. The erotic
nature image of the second stanza: "More crimson glow the hills/
Greeted by the blush of evening" ("Röter glänzen die Hügel,/Die
des Abends Erröten grüsst"), leads into the third stanza: "The
delights of the cup and the kisses of rosy maids/Await me there;
see, they beckon now" ("Becherfreude beim Kuss rosiger Mädchen-
schar/Harret meiner daselbst; sehet, sie winken schon"). The
parallelism of expectation, greeting and sensual pleasure is intensified by the parallelism of the color imagery.

There are a number of instances of Novalis' use of imagery in
the early poetry that point forward to his later practices. We have
observed a marked tendency on Novalis' part to express his
thoughts through images. The practice is marred at this stage by
extravagant hyperbole and too obvious striving for effect. It is

important to note, however, that this tendency, one of the most important aspects of much of Novalis' later work, has its beginnings early in his development. Certain important themes in his later work are to be met with in this period. A recurrent phrase in the early poetry—"taught by nature" ("von der Natur gelehrt") becomes one of the central themes of *Die Lehrlinge zu Sais*. The erotic quality of water, stressed in this same work and elsewhere, is depicted in the imagery of "Badelied" (I, 301). Novalis never loses his love of color imagery, so evident in his early poetry, and we have already remarked on his practice of building his images on the parallelism between nature and man's emotions. It is rather striking that in the early poetry of the poet best known for the blue flower there should be no flower image other than that of the conventional Anacreontic rose.

At this period Novalis' greatest need as an image-maker is for control of his remarkable imaginative powers. He has himself touched upon the weakness of his early imagery in "Klagen eines Jünglings" (I, 325 ff), where he says: "Ever fresh images crowd exuberantly/Upon me, dipped in attar of roses" ("Üppig drängen immer frische Bilder/Sich zu mir, in Rosenöl getaucht"). His images come to him too rapidly. He lacks both the power to mould them and the critical sense to discard the images too long steeped in the "attar of roses" of Anacreontic poetry.

A PERIOD OF TRANSITION (1795-1797)

In October 1794, after the completion of his university studies, Novalis entered public life as a minor official in Tennstedt in Thuringia. A month later, while traveling in his official capacity, he met and fell in love with Sophie von Kühn. For the next two and a half years, until the death of his fiancée in March 1797, Novalis' life centered on Sophie's home in Grüningen. Whatever posterity has made of the romance of Novalis and Sophie—there are those who scoff at the poet's love for this girl, only twelve years old when he first met her, as well as those who overestimate its significance to his poetry—there can be no doubt that Novalis' love was intense and that it had a sobering influence on him. The poetry of the Grüningen years has a marked aspect of transition. It is in these years that Novalis breaks with the conventionality of his early poetry and moves toward a style of his own and toward independence in choice and treatment of theme. The responsibilities of his new position and his love seem to have made Novalis a more reflective person and to have contributed to the maturing process that is discernible in his poetry. At the same time the discipline of the study of the sciences and philosophy, to which the poet applied himself diligently during these years, must have contributed to the development of his critical sense. A more important influence, however, were probably the criticisms of the Schlegels, with whom Novalis was by this time on intimate terms. Their more mature and objective criticism of his work must doubtless have enabled Novalis to see his poetry in a clearer light. Certainly the poems written in this period show greater evidence of self-discipline and self-criticism than anything he had previously produced.

The pious atmosphere of the *Herrnhut* [2] household around which Novalis' life revolved in these years would seem to have awakened a dormant religious sense in the poet. From this point he is fervent in his religious beliefs.[3] This ardor finds little immediate expression in his poetry, but it contributes to his turning from Anacreontic themes towards more serious subject matter. In all, this is a period in which Novalis expands his interests and the breadth of his experience, but it is also a time in which he is far less productive. Only eleven completed poems have survived from this period, and we have no indication that any others were written.[4] Yet a glance

---

[2] The name usually given in German to the Pietist sect, the Moravians, after the family seat of Count Zinzendorf who reconstituted in 1722 the sect originally founded in Bohemia in 1467. Novalis was himself raised in a *Herrnhut* family.

[3] *Cf.* Friedrich Schlegel to Caroline, August 2, 1796: "The very first day Hardenberg went to such extremes with his *Herrnhut* preachments that I should have liked to have left at once ... When I spoke above of *Herrnhut* preachments this was only the most convenient way of describing his absolute zealotry, for so far Hardenberg is completely free of the slightest trace of *Herrnhut* baseness" ("Gleich den ersten Tag hat mich Hardenberg mit der Herrnhüterei so weit gebracht, dass ich nur auf der Stelle hätte fortreisen mögen ... Wenn ich oben von der Herrnhüterei sprach, so wars nur der kürzeste Ausdruck für absolute Schwärmerei; denn noch ist Hardenberg ganz frei von dem leisesten Anstrich Herrnhüterischer Niederträchtigkeit").

[4] All the poems of this period are published by Kluckhohn, I, 335-347,

at these poems will suffice to show that Novalis is a much more competent poet than he was two or three years before. A more careful reading of them will reveal the characteristics that lead me to view this period as a period of transition.

Five of the Grüningen poems are purely occasional ones, written, one may be sure, to be read to Sophie's family. In them Novalis often resorts to the extravagent hyperbolic metaphor that mars so much of his earlier work. This is, perhaps, excusable if we remember that Novalis' audience would expect this type of imagery and that he was, after all, a young man seeking to impress his fiancée and her family with his talents. Interestingly enough, the classical references of the earlier poetry have been replaced by references to individual members of the Grüningen circle. While the allusions may be meaningless to the reader unfamiliar with the details of the poet's life, they have the virtue of being congruous to the poems' themes. There is, too, a marked decrease in the use of imagery in general. The Anacreontic images, for example, to which we have become accustomed in the earlier poetry are now conspicuously absent. Thus the poems do not have the crowded aspect that we remarked in the earlier poetry. Even in this occasional verse there is evidence of conscious application to the technical aspects of poetry that should have been revealing to those who criticized the Romantics for their lack of attention to form. The poem "Sonnabend" (I, 337 f) has a stanza structure which mirrors the composition of the theme. The first three stanzas describe the poet before he fell in love; the remaining three stanzas depict the changes wrought by love and lead up to the *pointe* of the introduction of Sophie's name. The poem is most remarkable, however, for its periphrasis. Eve is presented as "Father Adam's spouse," while everything the poet says of himself is expressed through metaphor and simile: "Am I still the one who . . . over all solemnity and care/Swung the light whip of joy . . . Who long ago in childhood's shoes/Left love's house of cards" ("Bin ich noch der, der . . . über allen Ernst und Sorgen/Der Freude leichte Geissel schwang . . . Der mit den Kinderschuhen lange/Der Liebe Kartenhaus verliess").

The remaining poems of this period are not so directly related to

---

under the heading "Grüningen." The two periods into which Kluckhohn divides Novalis' early poetry are based on biographical criteria.

the Grüningen group. There is no internal evidence in "Vergiss
mein nicht" (I, 335), for example, to link it with Sophie, though
one might justifiably assume that it is addressed to her. This poem
is remarkable for its simplicity. The language is well fitted to the
simple theme of undying love. There is no illegitimate reference
to disturb the poem and Novalis has been successful in eliminating
mere ornament from his verse. As a result this poem is superior
to any of his earlier love poetry. One of the most successful poems
written by Novalis before 1798 is "Walzer" (I, 336). It begins
"Waltzing down the paths of life" ("Hinunter die Pfade des Lebens
gedreht"), and the pronounced waltz rhythm is maintained throughout without any noticeable distortion of syntax. The waltz image,
which symbolizes both the transitory nature of life and happiness
and man's flight into sensual pleasure, is expanded in the following
verses: "Pause not, I beg you, until you must./Press the maidens
more firmly to your pounding heart/You know how fleeting are
youth and mirth" ("Pausiert nicht, ich bitt euch, solang es noch
geht./Drückt fester die Mädchen ans klopfende Herz/Ihr wisset,
wie flüchtig ist Jugend und Scherz"). Both in conception and
execution this is one of Novalis' most successful images to this
point in his development. Indeed, it is the first poem in which one
central image dominates the whole poem and in which the poem
grows from this image.

The one religious poem of this period points backward to the
way Novalis has come, but, at the same time, has thematic simi-
larity to his later religious lyrics. "Die Auferstehung" (I, 344 f)
begins on a hyperbolic tone: "Mountains exult, hills skip for joy,/
Breathe gladness, whatever lives" ("Berge jauchzet, Hügel hüpfet,/
Atme Freude, was da lebt"), and is reminiscent of "Gott" (I, 315):
"I sing anthems to God/With the flight of a lofty seraph . . ."
("Ich singe Gott im Hochgesang/Mit hohen Seraphs Flug . . .").
The metaphor of the poem marks, on occasion, a return to his
bombastic imitation of Klopstock's tone: "Angels marvel, Orions/
Thunder to Thee a song of praise ("Engel staunen, Orionen/
Donnern dir ein Loblied hin"). The themes of resurrection and
Christ's triumph over the horror of death are later developed in
both the *Hymnen an die Nacht* and the *Geistliche Lieder*, but the
mode of expression is not yet that of the mature works.

The most satisfying of all Novalis' poems written before 1798 is the poem "Es kann kein Rausch sein" (I, 346 f). Internal evidence suggests that it was written shortly after the death of the poet's fiancée in March 1797. In both the reflective nature of its theme and in its mode of composition the poem is markedly different from any of his earlier poems. For the first time Novalis uses the rhetorical question, which he later exploits in *Hymnen an die Nacht*, as an important structural element—and uses it successfully. For the first time, too, we find an image in the poem which reflects the poet's special scientific interests: "In this mad world approached too near/To my magnetic sphere" ("In dieser tollen Welt zu nah an/Meinen magnetischen Kreis gekommen"). The poem consists of eight stanzas, each stanza expressing one main thought, but the poem is remarkable for the way in which one dominant image runs throughout, knitting together the constituent ideas. From the initial image, "It cannot be intoxication" ("Es kann kein Rausch sein"), there develops a pattern of complementing imagery: "Could perfect knowledge/Of moral grace really be intoxication? . . . Is this intoxication too? Then there would remain for sobriety,/For truth, only the mask, the sound and the/Feeling of emptiness . . . Some day mankind will be what Sophie/Is now for me—perfect—moral grace/Then no longer will its higher consciousness/Be confused with the vapors of wine" ("Ein Rausch wär wirklich sittlicher Grazie/Vollendetes Bewusstsein? . . . Ist dies auch Rausch? so bliebe der Nüchternheit,/Der Wahrheit nur die Maske, der Ton und das/Gefühl der Leere . . . Einst wird die Menschheit sein, was Sophie mir/Jetzt ist—vollendet—sittliche Grazie—/Dann wird ihr höheres Bewusstsein/Nicht mehr verwechselt mit Dunst des Weines"). The development of one central image to its resolution in the final stanza of the poem shows that Novalis has rid himself of the major weakness of his earlier imagery, his fault of ruining one image by smothering it with another.

In general, then, this brief account of the Grüningen poetry indicates that Novalis has almost completely overcome the worst faults of his earlier work. He has put behind him conventional Anacreontic imagery and illegitimate reference. No longer merely ornament, imagery has achieved a definite function in his poetry. He has rid himself of his practice of intensifying one image by another; instead, he reinforces the image from within itself. His imagery is now, for the most part, controlled, and is better integrated with the theme and composition of the poem. It does not stand completely in isolation and is therefore more effective. Novalis is no longer the slave of his models, even though instances where he imitates are apparent. It is obvious that he has now developed a critical sense and that in choice and use of imagery his skill more nearly equals that of his use of meter and rhyme. Imagery continues to be the means of expression to which he most naturally turns, but he is no longer entirely dependent on other poets for his images. However, at this point in his development Novalis has not created an imagery or a symbolism peculiarly his own.

CHAPTER III

DIE LEHRLINGE ZU SAIS

It was with unaccountable suddenness that in 1798, just three years before he died of tuberculosis, Novalis decided to devote himself exclusively to literature. Hitherto the greater part of his time and efforts had been consumed by his study of the sciences and philosophy. In the short years that remained to him Novalis worked feverishly at his productions, taking up one project only to lay it aside in favor of another. The first of these, *Die Lehrlinge zu Sais,* was to remain a fragment at his death. Novalis' first mention of his nascent novel—"I have made a start . . . with the title 'The Apprentice of Saïs' " ("Ich habe . . . einen Anfang unter dem Titel 'Der Lehrling zu Sais' ")—came in February 1798, when he informed August Wilhelm Schlegel, "In the future I shall make poetry my only pursuit" ("Künftig treib ich nichts als Poesie" [IV, 229]). We may surmise, both from evidence in the surviving text and from the poet's own statements, that he planned a novel of broad scope. A letter to Friedrich Schlegel in January, 1800 (IV, 324 ff) indicates that Novalis temporarily interrupted his work on this novel to devote himself to *Heinrich von Ofterdingen,* while a letter to Tieck (IV, 329 ff) suggests that it was to be taken up again as soon as *Ofterdingen* was finished. At the same time he indicates that he has modified his original plans for the work. Now he tells Tieck, "It is to be a truly symbolic novel of nature ("Es soll ein echt-sinnbildlicher Naturroman werden"), though earlier he had spoken of "fragments—only all of them having reference to nature" ("Fragmente—nur alle in Beziehung auf Natur" [IV, 229]). This latter statement, however, was made at a time when Novalis had scarcely begun work on his project. There is adequate evidence in the fragment as it has survived to show that the work soon was to assume the form of a symbolic novel. One change in plan is immediately apparent. Novalist first referred to the work as "Der Lehrling zu Sais," so that the adoption of the plural form in the title suggests the broadening of the scope of the novel as it was written. Other indications of the author's plan can be found in those of his notes that obviously refer to this work,[1] though caution must be exercised in interpreting these. Lacking conclusive evidence, we cannot establish whether these are notes made by the author before the actual composition of the two chapters that were completed, or whether they are plans for revision. If they are assumed categorically to be the latter, they may, in fact, lead to a misinterpretation of the text as we have it. In any case, we must bear in mind that we have before us but a fragment of a larger work and, indeed, many elements in the text assume greater significance if this fact is not forgotten.

With any fragmentary production there is a strong temptation to postulate the final form of the work. In *Die Lehrlinge zu Sais* Novalis has given us many clues to his intent. Particularly valid indications are to be found in the fairy tale of Hyazinth and Rosenblüte in the second chapter of the fragment. This story, though often studied in isolation from the rest of the work, is incontrovertibly linked to the larger context, particularly, as will be shown later, by its imagery. It is the thesis of this study that the fairy tale presents the theme of the larger work in essence, and that "Märchen" and larger work complement each other. Correct interpretation of one without the other, I shall endeavor to show, is impossible.

The work, as we know it today, consists of only two chapters. The first, entitled "The Apprentice" ("Der Lehrling"), reveals the thoughts of the central figure of the novel, the apprentice of the chapter's title. The second chapter, "Nature" ("Die Natur"), has less apparent unity than the first and falls into four main parts: the apprentice's thoughts as he ponders on man's relationship to nature; the fairy tale of Hyazinth and Rosenblüte; the conversations between three travelers and a handsome youth; and the final speech of the apprentice's teacher. The unity of the chapter lies in the fact that nature, as its title suggests, is the theme to which all these elements have reference. The skillful composition of both chapters,

---

[1] Listed together by Kluckhohn as "Paralipomena," I, 41.

and the importance of imagery in them, will become apparent in our analysis of the text.

Novalis sets his story at Saïs in Egypt, where in pre-Christian days there was a large temple and flourishing cult of Isis. The figure of Isis, the veiled goddess on whose face no mortal might look, is well known in Western literature. The Egyptian cult of Isis was early woven into the Christian madonna cult after Herodotus had previously identified Isis with the Greek goddess of fertility and growth, Demeter. Plato recounts that it was from the priests at Saïs that Solon learned the secrets of man's prehistory and the myth of Atlantis. In Novalis' own day the figure of Isis appeared in Rosicrucian poetry, and Schiller used the image of the veiled goddess to symbolize ultimate truth in his poem "Das verschleierte Bild zu Sais." There is nothing, however, in Novalis' work, except the setting at Saïs, that has reference to Egypt or to the traditions of the cult. His work transcends both setting and tradition, neither of which is vital to his theme.

The first chapter of the fragment has a climactic structure. It begins with a broad statement of the theme of the apparent duality of man and nature and rises to the final paragraph in which this theme is expressed in symbol. The whole chapter, it becomes apparent, is an interior monologue, in which the apprentice, identified only by the title of the chapter, examines himself and his relationship to nature, to his teacher and to his fellow apprentices.

The opening paragraph expresses in three broad images the apprentice's view of man's existence, and we are thus presented immediately with the basic problem of the work. The first image depicts the diverse forms of man's existence in terms of paths taken through life: "Very different are the roads men take" ("Mannigfache Wege gehen die Menschen"). To this is contrasted the image of order and pattern in nature. Evidence of this order pattern, this great "cipher-writing" ("Chiffrenschrift"),[2] is to be found everywhere—"on wings, eggshells, in clouds, in the snow, in crystals and in rock formations ... in the filings around the magnet" ("auf Flügeln, Eierschalen, in Wolken, im Schnee, in Kristallen und in Steinbildungen, ... in den Feilspänen um den

---

[2] Ernst Robert Curtius, *Europäische Literatur und Lateinisches Mittelalter* (Bern, 1948), pp. 349f, points to the origin of this metaphor in Islamic-Spanish culture.

Magnet her"). For the apprentice, man's effort to understand this language of nature is the problem of existence: "In them we divine the key to this magic writing, the grammar of it, but what we sense refuses to take on definite form and seems not to want to become a master key" ("In ihnen ahndet man den Schlüssel dieser Wunderschrift, die Sprachlehre derselben, allein die Ahndung will sich selbst in keine feste Formen fügen, und scheint kein höherer Schlüssel werden zu wollen"). When men seek to grasp the forms of this writing, it seems as though an alkahest, that fabled universal solvent of the alchemists, had been poured over their senses: "Only for the moment do their wishes and ideas seem to condense. Thus their presentiments take shape, but after a brief moment everything again swims before their eyes as it had done before" ("Nur augenblicklich scheinen ihre Wünsche, ihre Gedanken sich zu verdichten. So entstehen ihre Ahndungen, aber nach kurzen Zeiten schwimmt alles wieder, wie vorher, vor ihren Blicken"). This image of elusive fluidity, I would suggest, is the implicit expression of the dominant symbol of the work—the veil image. Between man and nature, Novalis indicates, there is a veil that cuts man off from the intercourse with nature he had once enjoyed. It is to the raising of this veil, as the climax of this chapter shows, that the apprenticeship of the hero is directed.

The apprentice—for now we learn that these are *his* thoughts— is disturbed by the recollection of a voice of pessimism that doubted man's ability ever to understand the language of nature. His own doubts are dispelled, however, by a voice of faith and assurance that sees truth in man as a chord from the harmony of the universe. This leads the apprentice to think of his teacher—identified only as "der Lehrer"—for the teacher sees the great ordered pattern in nature and can read her writing: "he knows how to put together the elements that are everywhere scattered" ("er versteht die Züge zu versammeln, die überall zerstreut sind"). Images of light reveal the teacher's ardent devotion to nature and the apprehension by his pupils of the message he seeks to impart to them: "His eyes catch fire with a peculiar light when the noble rune lies before us and he peers into our eyes to see whether in us has risen the constellation that makes the figure visible and understandable" ("Ein eignes Licht entzündet sich in seinen Blicken, wenn vor uns nun die hohe Rune liegt, und er in unsern Augen späht, ob auch

in uns aufgegangen ist das Gestirn, das die Figur sichtbar und
verständlich macht"). The teacher has set himself the task of
revealing to others some of the secrets he has learned in the course
of his own development, a development made vivid by the images
in which the apprentice recalls it. (At the same time, the naive,
intuitive nature of the youth himself is revealed through his use of
literal images and simple metaphor.) From a childlike wish to
reproduce the pattern in nature, the teacher passed to the stage of
self-observation: "He listened carefully to his feelings and his
thoughts" ("Auf sein Gemüt und seine Gedanken lauschte er sorg-
sam"). Observation led him to creative imitation—"he saw how
the structure of the earth was executed in layers and strata of
variegated color and he pressed clay into the form of strange rock
formations" ("sah wie in Bänken und in bunten Schichten der Erde
Bau vollführt war, und drückte Ton in sonderbare Felsenbilder")
—and his appreciation of the constant order in nature was followed
by the realization of inner harmony. This, in turn, gave him the
power to objectivate his thoughts in images and to synthesize his
impressions: "he heard, saw, felt and thought simultaneously" ("er
hörte, sah, tastete und dachte zugleich"). He rejoiced in his power
to associate apparent antitheses, to see one form in another: "Now
for him the stars were people, now people were stars, stars animals,
clouds were plants" ("Bald waren ihm die Sterne Menschen, bald
die Menschen Sterne, die Sterne Tiere, die Wolken Pflanzen").
From this stage he passed to the stage of independent creation:
"thus himself searched the strings for notes and arpeggios" ("griff so
selbst in den Saiten nach Tönen und Gängen"), a musical image
which is linked in its reference with the earlier image of the
harmony of the universe, "des Weltalls Symphonie."

What the teacher's development has been beyond this point, the
apprentices have not been told. The teacher has left them to discover the final secret for themselves. The thoughts of the apprentice
now carry him to his fellow apprentices and we are shown that
there are many ways in which the apprenticeship to nature may
be served. (Throughout the work the diversity of man's approaches
to nature is stressed and it is this emphasis, I suggest, that led
Novalis to adopt the plural form in the title of his work.) Several
of the apprentices have left the teacher to return to their former
pursuits, the implication being that, for many, the apprenticeship

to nature is too demanding. Others have been sent out as disciples to preach the new gospel of nature. One of these, clearly a Messiah figure, was no doubt intended to play a major rôle in the dénouement of the novel. Though this apprentice was only a child the teacher wanted to hand over the instruction to him. " 'Some day he will return,' said the teacher, 'and dwell among us; then our instruction will cease' " (" 'Einst wird es wiederkommen,' sagte der Lehrer, 'und unter uns wohnen, dann hören die Lehrstunden auf' "). Another apprentice, formerly clumsy and inept, had been sent out as the child's companion. The chance discovery of a wonderful stone—an experience comparable to the experience of Grace in the Christian religion—had changed this clumsy apprentice and fitted him to go out with the child.[3] For the other apprentices, too, the sight of this stone, which seems in the work to have thaumaturgical qualities, was like a revelation of divine truth.

The apprentice's thoughts now turn to himself. The structure of the chapter illustrates what the apprentice says of himself: "Everything leads me back to my inner self" ("Mich führt alles in mich selbst zurück"). He feels himself less fitted for his task than his fellows, yet he finds strength in the fact that the teacher understands him and leaves him to his own thoughts. He rejoices in the natural objects in the temple,[4] but he sees them only as the outer symbol of a divine image that itself constantly occupies his thoughts. The objects about him, he feels, are signposts, pointing the way he must go: "It is as though they were to guide me to the place where, in deep sleep, stands the virgin for whom my spirit yearns" ("Es ist, als sollten sie den Weg mir zeigen, wo in tiefem Schlaf die Jungfrau steht, nach der mein Geist sich sehnt"). The teacher has told him nothing of this; it is an intuitive feeling for a secret he cannot reveal, even to the teacher. His deep faith in reaching his goal—and some intuition tells him that his final goal is to be the

---

[3] Cf. "Paralipomena" 4: "The child and his St. John. The Messiah of nature" ("Das Kind und sein Johannes. Der Messias der Natur")—an obvious reference to the two figures of this paragraph.

[4] Novalis obviously imagines the temple as a museum of natural history, for which, as part of their training, the apprentices collect and arrange specimens. Both the teacher and his pupils display a religious reverence for stones, rocks and plants.

temple at Saïs—lets him accept the burdens of his apprenticeship. Through this faith everything becomes familiar. That he does not understand the teacher does not depress him, for the teacher has emphasized that each must follow his own course, "because every new path goes through new lands, and each one finally leads back to these dwellings, to this sacred home" ("weil jeder neue Weg durch neue Länder geht, und jeder endlich zu diesen Wohnungen, zu dieser heiligen Heimat wieder führet"). (The implicit image contained in these words is second in importance only to the veil image. It is not, as I shall demonstrate more conclusively later, a circle image but one of a spiral that ends essentially at the starting point but at a higher level, for the individual is purified through his pilgrimage back to nature.) Then, with great emotional emphasis, the youth proclaims his faith in achieving his goal: "Thus I too will describe my figure, and if no mortal, according to that inscription, may raise the veil, then we must seek to become immortals; he who does not seek to raise it is no true apprentice of Saïs" ("Auch ich will also meine Figur beschreiben, und wenn kein Sterblicher, nach jener Inschrift dort, den Schleier hebt, so müssen wir Unsterbliche zu werden suchen; wer ihn nicht heben will, ist kein echter Lehrling zu Sais").

Only now, in this final poignant statement by the youth, do we learn what the final goal of the apprenticeship is—the raising of the veil that hides the goddess from man's eyes. This is the theme of the work in symbol, but what goddess and veil symbolize only becomes clear in the fairy tale of Hyazinth and Rosenblüte. At this point goddess and veil are images rather than symbols. It is only when we meet these images again in the "Märchen" that they assume full symbolic character, linking action at two different levels. This correspondence between the imagery of the fairy tale and the larger work, more than anything else, gives the work its symbolic character. It is through these images, as they complement each other, that we are led to the heart of the poet's meaning.

In the second chapter, "Die Natur," Novalis continues to portray his apprentice's thoughts, though in this case they are presented as a series of voices to which the apprentice listens. As in the first chapter the author's mode of presentation is not at once apparent. Only later do we learn that the apprentice is listening to these voices. The history of man's relationship to nature is presented in succinct form[5] and Novalis takes us rapidly through the various approaches of man to nature, using imagery to make palpable the ideas discussed. The accounts of modern philosophic systems, obvious anachronisms if the setting of the work is taken literally, show that Novalis had no particular era or country in mind as the setting of his work. Early man is shown to have been one with nature, and it is man's later development of his individual intellectual faculties that has caused him to be divorced from nature. Only after man's separation from nature did he feel the need to analyze his relationship to her. The earliest scientific approaches to nature show that man first interpreted the world in two broad ways, either in terms of "predominating substances"—"in einer Hauptmasse der wirklichen Dinge"—or as the "invention of an unknown intellect"—"in dem erdichteten Gegenstand eines unbekannten Sinns." A later approach was that of the atomist: "He sought to untie the knot through a kind of amalgamation, by beginning with tiny bodies of fixed shape, which were, however, inconceivably small . . ." ("Er versuchte den Knoten durch eine Art von Vereinigung zu lösen, indem er die ersten Anfänge zu festen, gestalteten Körperchen machte, die er jedoch über allen Begriff klein annahm . . ."). To this approach was joined that of interpreting the world in terms of natural forces, although, Novalis suggests, man had come much closer to the truth in earlier, anthropomorphic approaches that interpreted the world in terms of human agencies. For Novalis, poetry has best succeeded in revealing nature to man—a thesis which runs through the work. He points to myth and fairy tale as the earliest and most natural interpretation of nature, this claim pointing up the significance of the fairy tale within his own work. His statement that nature is best understood as a human being leads to a long and beautifully developed personification image in which are portrayed the relationships of poet and scientist to nature. While the scientist has been surgeon and father-confessor to nature, it is the poet who has understood her and enjoyed her love: "Thus she enjoyed divine moments with the poet, and called the naturalist to her only when she was ill and conscience-stricken" ("So genoss sie himmlische

---

[5] This account has, as will be pointed out later, a function in the novel beyond that of showing, as it does, how man has failed to understand nature through scientific approaches.

Stunden mit dem Dichter, und lud den Naturforscher nur dann ein, wenn sie krank und gewissenhaft war"). Poetry can reveal nature as a living creature, while science can at best expose her individual parts.

The apprentice's thoughts now turn to what nature can mean for man. Again the infinite variety of nature and the diversity of man's approaches to her are stressed when Novalis says that nature can be all things to all men. To the child she is childlike, to the god godlike. Once more imagery makes these relationships palpable. Some seek beyond nature for the old and familiar, others for a new world, while few are content to grasp her as she really is. Some, again, see in nature only "a gay kitchen and larder" ("eine lustige Küche und Speisekammer"), while for others she has become a religion that has given meaning and purpose to their lives. Great among these lovers of nature are those who have sought to give form to a nature that has become wild and inaccessible as a result of her divorce from man. Among these Novalis characteristically ranks the miner with the musician, the farmer with the architect: "As companions they shared in the great work, some seeking to awaken the muted and lost tones in the air and forests, others ... building dwellings again from beautiful rocks, bringing the buried treasures from the caverns of the earth back to the surface ... opening the earth to the life-bringing touch of procreative air and kindling light" ("Sie teilten sich gesellig in das grosse Werk, die einen suchten die verstummten und verlornen Töne in Luft und Wäldern zu erwecken, andre ... bauten schönere Felsen zu Wohnungen wieder, brachten die verborgenen Schätze aus den Grüften der Erde wieder ans Licht ... öffneten die Erde den belebenden Berührungen der zeugenden Luft und des zündenden Lichts"). Through the efforts of such individuals the apprentice foresees the gradual return of the Golden Age when man and nature were one: "when she dwelt among them and men were made immortal through intimacy with the divine" ("als sie unter ihnen wohnte und ein himmlischer Umgang die Menschen zu Unsterblichen machte"). This description of man's state in the Golden Age[6] recalls the words of the apprentice at the close of Chapter I:

[6] The imagery in which Novalis here embodies his concept of the returned Golden Age is remarkably similar to the imagery of the *Hymnen an die Nacht* in which is depicted the eventual reunion of physical and

"and if no mortal, according to that inscription, may raise the veil, then we must seek to become immortals. . . ."

Although the apprentice goes on to dwell on the characteristics that stamp the true lover of nature—diligent observation, humility, naïveté, faith—he realizes that, for some, nature is irreconcilably hostile to man, and that they seek escape from a nature they regard as a "dreadful mill of death." Better, for them, mass suicide than the danger of madness to which their contact with nature constantly exposes them! For these, nature is a constant threat to man's reason, so that association with nature can only drag man down through the successive levels of beast, plant, rock, and storm to final destruction. Even bolder men than they regard nature as a force against which mankind must incessantly wage war, and for them the scientist is a hero who plunges into the abyss to save his fellows. Patience, faith and above all the freedom of the human will are the weapons by which they may conquer nature. The purer world lies within man himself, and in this assurance he may face the ardors of existence. The final voice in the apprentice's thoughts is that of the subjective idealist (perhaps Fichte), who refutes the foregoing arguments. For him, nature is the product of man's senses, and rational man recognizes this without fear. Man should honor nature as the symbol of himself, and by exercising his moral sense he will cause nature to bow to him.

The apprentice is confused by these conflicting theories and feels that each one has merit. Yet his doubts are gradually dispelled as his own faith reasserts itself. His reflections are interrupted, however, by the advent of a gay, young apprentice, who warns him of the dangers of introspection and meditation. There is a prophetic

---

spiritual worlds. Here we find, as in the *Hymnen an die Nacht,* light implicitly portrayed as a despotic king of the physical universe—"then the sun will lay down his harsh scepter" ("dann legt die Sonne ihren strengen Zepter nieder")—while the world becomes a place of reunion for people long parted and a source of new life: "in every grave stir newly glowing ashes, everywhere flames of life blaze up" ("in jedem Hügel regt sich neu erglimmende Asche, überall lodern Flammen des Lebens empor"). Both here and in the hymns eternity is envisioned as an everlasting dream, and it is in a dream-state that Hyazinth attains immortality in the "Märchen." This correspondence suggests the existence of a fixed symbolic pattern in the poet's mind, and that such a pattern did, in fact, exist will be apparent in our discussion of his other works.

touch, too, in the words of this disciple of feeling when he says: "Poor fellow, you have never been in love! At the first kiss a new world will be revealed to you . . ." ("Du hast noch nicht geliebt, du Armer, beim ersten Kuss wird eine neue Welt dir aufgetan . . ."). Then, to illustrate his point, he tells the story of Hyazinth and Rosenblüte.

It is significant that Novalis has chosen this point in his novel for the telling of his delightful "Märchen." The apprentice's reflections have shown him to be inclined to introspection and dialectic thought processes. They have shown us, too, how far he has yet to go before he reaches his goal. Though possessed of intuitive understanding and a naive capacity to see relationships and correspondences (as his use of imagery demonstrates), he is inclined to value thought above feeling. Now, when we read the description of Hyazinth at the beginning of the fairy tale, we are at once struck by the parallel between Hyazinth and the speculative apprentice. What is said of Hyazinth could equally well be said of him: "He fretted incessantly about nothing at all, always walked quietly by himself, sat alone while the others played and were gay, and abandoned himself to strange ideas" ("Er grämte sich unaufhörlich um nichts und wieder nichts, ging immer still für sich hin, setzte sich einsam, wenn die andern spielten und fröhlich waren, und hing seltsamen Dingen nach"). A few years before, we are told, Hyazinth had been gay and happy in his love for the beautiful Rosenblüte and had been blissfully in harmony with his surroundings. (The flower-names chosen by Novalis emphasize the oneness with nature of Hyazinth and Rosenblüte in this Golden Age idyll, as does their ability to converse with animals, plants and natural objects). But a change was wrought in Hyazinth's existence with the advent of a mysterious stranger with enthralling stories of strange lands and people. When the stranger departed, he left behind "a little book that nobody could read" ("ein Büchelchen . . ., das kein Mensch lesen konnte"). It was then that Hyazinth forgot the beauty of his former existence and cut himself off from Rosenblüte. It was then that he became the confused, melancholy creature described above. But one day he came home "and seemed as if reborn." An old woman in the woods had burned his book and told him how he might be restored to his former state. He is unable to describe his emotions at this point: "whenever I seek to think back on the old days more powerful thoughts immediately intervene;[7] my peace of mind has gone, and with it my heart and love . . ." ("wenn ich an die alten Zeiten zurückdenken will, so kommen gleich mächtigere Gedanken dazwischen, die Ruhe ist fort, Herz und Liebe mit . . ."). He knows he must go and seek the veiled virgin: "For her my heart is inflamed . . ." ("Nach der ist mein Gemüt entzündet . . ."). Through many strange lands Hyazinth wanders, asking and seeking for the goddess, Isis, the veiled virgin. As he progresses, his inner mood changes and he is filled with a "sweet yearning." [8] His surroundings become more and more familiar as he approaches his goal. He meets familiar forms and faces and finally reaches the temple of the virgin, "the dwelling place of the eternal seasons" ("die Behausung der ewigen Jahreszeiten"). Here Hyazinth falls asleep, "because only the dream might conduct him into the holy of holies" "'weil ihn nur der Traum in das Allerheiligste führen durfte"). In the dream state he passes through numerous chambers, filled with strangely familiar objects: "Everything seemed so familiar, and yet it appeared in a splendor never seen before" ("Es dünkte ihm alles so bekannt und doch in niegesehener Herrlichkeit"). Finally he stands before the virgin and raises the veil, to find Rosenblüte beneath it.

The many parallels between the fairy tale and the larger work, particularly in imagery, justify our seeing the fairy tale as the larger work in essence, as the allegorical presentation of the theme of the whole novel as Novalis planned it. The fairy tale assumes its allegorical character through the parallels between it and the larger work.[9] While the series of images it presents, taken in iso-

---

[7] Again, the implicit veil image.

[8] "Eine süsse Sehnsucht"—defined throughout the work as the most vital requisite for the true lover of nature.

[9] The isolation of the fairy tale from its context has led to a variety of interpretations. Thus, Luitgart Albrecht, *Der magische Idealismus in Novalis' Märchentheorie und Märchendichtung* (Hamburg, 1948), p. 83, sees the tale as an allegory of the realization of the highest state of self-consciousness. Friedrich Hiebel, *Novalis. Der Dichter der blauen Blume* (Bern, 1951), p. 103, claims "The images of the fable have no allegoric significance" ("Die Bilder des Märchens haben keine allegorische Bedeutung"), but goes on to give an allegoric interpretation which takes no note of the parallels to which attention is drawn in this study. *Cf.* also H. W. Hewett-Thayer, *Hoffmann: Author of "The Tales"* (Princeton, 1948), p. 216: "Novalis left the exquisite little tale of Hyacinth and Rosenblüte

lation, hint at allegory, their true meaning becomes clear only as they are related to the images of the larger work. The "Märchen" deepens the meaning of the images of *Die Lehrlinge zu Sais*, making them symbolic, while at the same time elements of the larger context supply the key to the allegoric meaning of the fairy tale. The "Märchen," of course, points beyond the fragment to the final realization of the apprentice's goal. An analysis of the action and imagery of the fairy tale within the context of the fragment accordingly reveals what Novalis planned as the action of the completed novel.

The idyllic state of Hyazinth and Rosenblüte, before Hyazinth's falling victim to the tales of the stranger, is clearly that enjoyed by mankind in the Golden Age to which there is so often reference in the fragment. Hyazinth is turned into an unhappy, lonely and dissatisfied creature through his thirst for knowledge—knowledge, which, if we may identify the sum total of our scientific knowledge with the illegible book of the stranger, can only keep us from nature. For Hyazinth a veil had been drawn between himself and his former idyllic state. It is only through a chance contact with nature (his encounter with the old woman in the woods),[10] that he realizes what he has lost. Hyazinth's first step towards recapturing his lost bliss is the burning of the book, an act symbolic of his renunciation of scientific knowledge, before beginning his long pilgrimage back to nature. As Hyazinth progressed towards his goal he met familiar forms and faces; we recall how the apprentice, too, had found that everything became familiar when his thoughts were occupied with the divine virgin. Finally Hyazinth entered the temple of the goddess—"the dwelling place of the eternal seasons" (the symbol, one assumes, of the hidden secrets of nature)—but it was in a dream state that he approached the virgin. If it were

---

without a 'moral' though an explanation, albeit a metaphysical one, may be found in a verse posthumously published. . . ." Hewett-Thayer apparently refers to an aphorism incorporated in the "Paralipomena" by Kluckhohn, (I, 41): "One succeeded—he raised the veil of the goddess of Sais—But what did he see? He saw—wonder of wonders—himself" ("Einem gelang es—er hob den Schleier der Göttin zu Sais—Aber was sah er? Er sah —Wunder des Wunders—sich selbst"). See below, n. 11, for a discussion of this aphorism in relation to the text.

[10] This may be compared with the chance discovery of the stone and its effect on the clumsy apprentice in Chapter I. *Cf.* above, p. 34.

assumed that the sleep into which Hyazinth falls is the sleep of death, the implication would be that the Golden Age can be regained only in an afterlife. Yet, although Hyazinth never awakens from his dream state, he lives on with Rosenblüte and has many children. We must refer to the larger context to explain this dream state in which Hyazinth wins immortality. The apprentice asserted in the first chapter that no mortal may raise the veil and that the true apprentice must therefore seek immortality. We learn later that in the Golden Age man was made immortal through his intercourse with nature: "when she dwelt among them and men were made immortal through intimacy with the divine." It is this immortality, clearly, that is attained by Hyazinth, a regaining of the naive, pure state of innocence that existed before man's separation from nature. It is the return of man to his point of origin, as the familiar surroundings (seen in new splendor) and the discovery of Rosenblüte beneath the veil indicate. Yet Novalis' theme is more than Rousseauism. Hyazinth recaptures the Golden Age through love, for it is his beloved Rosenblüte who is the final secret of the holy of holies and in whose presence he wins immortality. The mystic union of man and nature is accomplished only through love, after the veil, the last vestige of the "culture" that has hidden nature from man, has been removed. Implicit too, in the discovery of Rosenblüte beneath the veil, is that Hyazinth regains what he has, essentially, always possessed, for Rosenblüte has never ceased to love him. Nature is neither hostile nor lost to man, but only concealed from him by a veil of his own making. In this sense, Hyazinth, indeed, returns to his point of origin,[11] but because he is

---

[11] Fritz Strich, *Deutsche Klassik und Romantik,* 4th ed. (Bern, 1949), p. 90, indicates that the idea of "going home" was a dominant idea of Novalis' day. Alexander Gode-Von Aesch, *Natural Science in German Romanticism* (New York, 1941), p. 112, states: "The romantic motif of going home is the motif of finding one's real self." Gode-Von Aesch's interpretation of this motif in Novalis' poetry may have been influenced by an aphorism of Novalis, thought by Kluckhohn, Albrecht and others to have direct reference to this fairy tale: "One succeeded—he raised the veil of the goddess of Sais—But what did he see? He saw—wonder of wonders—himself." Irving Babbitt, *Rousseau and Romanticism* (Boston & New York, 1919), p. 226, says of the discovery of Rosenblüte and of this aphorism, which he regards as an alternative ending for the fairy tale: "The two endings are in substance the same." I cannot, in light of my interpretation of the imagery, accept the notion that Hyazinth's discovery

in the dream state (and hence immortal) he is at a higher level. The figure he describes[12] is, therefore, not a circle, but a spiral. When man regains the Golden Age it will be at a higher level for having consciously sought to regain it, for having, like Hyazinth, passed through the purifying process of his pilgrimage, filled with that indefinable "sweet yearning" to which Novalis so often alludes in this work.

We may, then, following the action of the fairy tale, postulate the action of the novel itself. The apprentice will follow the spiral path taken by Hyazinth. Although as yet caught up in man's effort to grasp nature through thought, he has nevertheless realized the existence of the veil. Like Hyazinth, he sees the image of the veiled virgin always before him. What his course will be we may surmise from the "Märchen." His path will take him through many lands, but eventually he will return, as the teacher has prophesied, to the temple at Saïs, "to these dwellings, to this sacred home." Like the "dwelling place of the eternal seasons" of the fairy tale, the temple at Saïs houses the veiled goddess, and its rooms, filled with the objects collected by the apprentices, will take on new splendor and significance on the apprentice's return. It is here, at his starting point, even as he himself had felt, that the apprentice will raise the veil and through love recapture that state of innocence and bliss that characterized man in the Golden Age.[13]

---

of Rosenblüte beneath the veil represents his attainment to self-knowledge, except in so far as the symbolic value of the act for the larger work—the reunion of man and nature—makes of the apparent duality of man and nature the unity which, in Novalis' eyes, the two actually represent. In this sense the attainment to full knowledge of nature is tantamount to the attainment to full knowledge of self. I must insist, however, that to see in Hyazinth's discovery of Rosenblüte only the finding of self is to destroy much of the symbolic value of the image.

[12] Cf. the apprentice's "Thus I too will describe my figure," above, p. 35.

[13] An interesting parallel may be drawn between the implicit argument advanced by Novalis and the view put forward by Heinrich von Kleist in his essay, "Über das Marionettentheater." Novalis implies that the state of naïveté and intuitive knowledge attained by man in the new Golden Age will be superior to that of the original Golden Age for man's having consciously sought this condition. In the closing paragraphs of his essay Kleist suggests the possibility of attainment to an innocent grace that knows no self-consciousness, with the implication, again, that such a state, consciously sought, is at a higher level than the purely natural condition.

What progress there is in the action of the novel in the remainder of the fragment is apparent only if we keep the "Märchen" before us. At the close of the tale the two apprentices leave and we hear the voices of nature, represented by the voices of the natural objects within the temple. (The pain and grief they express result from the arbitrary fashion in which they have been arranged.) Nature laments the fact that man has been separated from her—again musical images represent nature's ordered pattern, while man's failure to apprehend her harmony is depicted through his creation only of dissonance—and that he has forgotten the happiness they shared when they were one, "as in the Golden Age of long ago, as he rightly calls it" ("wie ehemals in der goldnen Zeit, wie er sie mit Recht nennt"). It is man's desire for knowledge that has led to his divorce from nature—"His desire to become God has separated him from us; he seeks what we can neither know nor sense" ("Seine Begierde, Gott zu werden, hat ihn von uns getrennt, er sucht, was wir nicht wissen und ahnden können")—and the voice of nature supports the claim of the gay apprentice that it is through feeling and not through thought that nature can be revealed to man: "Thought is only feeling's dream, feeling that has expired, a pallid and feeble life" ("Das Denken ist nur ein Traum des Fühlens, ein erstorbenes Fühlen, ein blassgraues und schwaches Leben"). The voice of nature thus complements the thesis of the "Märchen" that man's emotions, not his intellect, will lead him back to nature: "through feeling would return the old days for which he yearns" ("durch das Gefühl würde die alte, ersehnte Zeit zurückkommen"). At the same time Novalis makes clear his attitude towards the arguments that now ensue between a group of travelers and a handsome youth by revealing through these voices his belief in the oneness of man and nature and in the superiority of feeling to thought.

The arrival of the travelers at the temple is a step forward in the action of the novel. They, we may be sure, are to play something of the rôle in the larger work that the mysterious stranger played in the "Märchen." We learn that they are scientists seeking the traces of a lost race to whose high culture we owe most of our tools and knowledge, a reference, perhaps, to the legend of Atlantis. Later they obtain permission to stay for a few days at the temple, where they hope to gain information from the archives

about the language of that race. Like Hyazinth's strange visitor,
they tell stories of strange lands and people. We may assume that
the apprentice will for a while follow them in their search until
some contact with nature comparable to Hyazinth's encounter with
the old woman in the woods will reawaken his memories of the
virgin and turn him back to his true path. The greater part of the
remainder of the fragment consists of conversations between three
of the travelers and the handsome youth, whose figurative language
and emotional statements contrast sharply with the rational approach of the travelers. The views put forward by these scientists
are largely restatements of the problems with which the speculative
apprentice had earlier wrestled. Through their arguments are again
revealed the limitations of the nonpoetic approaches to nature. It
will be remembered that the apprentice had felt there was merit in
each of the various philosophic systems on which he had pondered;
in the travelers, therefore, we see a danger to the apprentice. Although he does not hear their arguments at this point, he is present
when they recount their visits to other lands; one may therefore
surmise that the apprentice is to have difficulty in resisting their
ideas. The conversations of the travelers and the youth fall into
two parts, each rising to a climax at which the youth, significantly,
has the last word. Again the youth's statements amplify the theme
of the fairy tale, the thesis that love is the key to man's final union
with nature. For the youth, the champion of poetry and feeling,
man and nature are one; for the traveler-scientists man and nature
are essentially a duality.

The first traveler, we may say, represents the viewpoint of
Kantian Idealism in his questioning of man's ability ever to pene-
trate beyond nature's outer garment. For him, the human ego
and man's freedom of will are all-important. Man's first task is to
know himself and from this he may proceed to the analysis of the
sensory reactions associated with certain phenomena. This scientist
sees man's highest form of activity in the evocation of sensory
reactions independent of stimuli—the evocation of the "ideal"
form. (We have already seen, however, in the teacher's development that this is but a stage beyond which man must progress.)

The second traveler may be said to represent a more cautious
scientific viewpoint. He is somewhat alarmed at the sweeping
generalizations of the first. He finds it difficult to interpret the

world as an entity; instead, he sees it in terms of monads, as "the point of contact and amalgamation of countless worlds" ("der Vereinigungs- und Berührungspunkt unzähliger Welten"). The third traveler, an eclectic who optimistically welcomes any new system of thought, boldly dismisses the objections of the second and proclaims with emphasis that a future historian of nature will select what is best in all systems and thereby produce a grand system that will enable us to understand nature.

The youth does not rely upon systems of thought but upon feeling. For him, nature is a great emotional being, attuned to man's soul. Only poets, he claims, have fully understood her and recaptured "all the bliss of the Golden Age." In figurative images he seeks to express the necessary existence of a deep emotional relationship between man and nature and is carried away by the fervor of his expression: "The wind is a movement of air which may have many external causes, but is it not more than this to a lonely heart filled with yearning when it whistles by, blowing from climes that he loves and seeming with a thousand dark melancholy tones to dissolve his quiet pain in one deep, melodic sigh of all nature?" ("Der Wind ist eine Luftbewegung, die manche äussere Ursachen haben kann, aber ist er dem einsamen, sehnsuchtsvollen Herzen nicht mehr, wenn er vorüberläuft, von geliebten Gegenden herweht und mit tausend dunkeln, wehmütigen Lauten den stillen Schmerz in einen tiefen melodischen Seufzer der ganzen Natur aufzulösen scheint?"). In the youth's eyes, man and nature are parts of one whole, complementing each other's existence. It is a relationship which the youth claims can be comprehended only by a naive being.

Again the three travelers state their views, though their viewpoints, formerly opposed to each other, are now modified one by the other. The effect is like that of a musical composition, like point and counterpoint. The claims of philosophy and science are given a full hearing in the arguments of the travelers, but the third traveler, swayed by the youth's ardor, recognizes with a flash of intuition that lovers understand nature more fully than does the scientist. This admission evokes a final outburst from the youth, in which he makes clear the significance of love in man's relationship to nature. The love of which he speaks is a highly erotic passion, "that mighty emotion for which language has no names

but love and voluptuousness" [14] ("jenes mächtige Gefühl, wofür
die Sprache keine andere Namen als Liebe und Wollust hat"). It
is an emotion that he can describe only in images of flame and
fluid. For him, water is the erotic element. He lauds the ancients
who sought the source of life in water, though they spoke of a
"higher water" than "sea or well water." Few have divined the
secrets and the highest bliss of this medium, these "Urwässer," and
yet all pleasant emotions are the stirring of these "primeval waters"
within us. (That Novalis has here anticipated some of the teachings
of Freud need hardly be pointed out.) But the youth recognizes the
futility of trying to teach those who cannot feel this passion. They
can never understand the intimate, erotic relationship that exists
between nature and her lover: "In nature's embrace he feels as he
does at the bosom of his demure sweetheart, and to his sweetheart
alone, in sweet moments of intimacy, does he confide the insights
he has gained . . . His life will be a fund of pleasures, a succession
of delights, and his religion will be true and genuine naturalism"
("Er fühlt sich in ihr wie am Busen seiner züchtigen Braut und
vertraut auch nur dieser seine erlangten Einsichten in süssen ver-
traulichen Stunden . . . Sein Leben wird eine Fülle aller Genüsse,
eine Kette der Wollust und seine Religion der eigentliche, echte
Naturalismus sein").

This erotic prose-poem is really Novalis' last word in the
fragment. The final paragraph, in which the teacher, returning
with his apprentices, summarizes the qualities of the prophet of
nature, is essentially a restatement of ideas already expressed. He
stresses particularly that the qualities essential to the prophet of
nature—faith, reverence, diligence, naïveté—are not limited to any
class or age. The teacher's statements are, however, like the quiet
coda of a tempestuous orchestral movement. The dominant chord
of the chapter has been struck in the youth's hymn to love. It is
erotic love that is the secret of life and the key to man's mystic
union with nature: "Whose heart does not stir with leaping joy
when he feels nature's innermost life in all its fullness! when that
mighty emotion, for which language has no names but love and

---

[14] In some contexts the German "Wollust" does not have the erotic
connotation of the English "voluptuousness," which I have here used to
translate it. It may denote intense pleasure or delight. In this particular
context, however, the word seems clearly to have this erotic force.

voluptuousness, spreads through his being like a powerful, all-dissolving vapor and he sinks down, quivering with sweet anguish, into the dark seductive womb of nature, his poor self is consumed in the breaking waves of desire, and there remains nothing but a focal point of immeasurable procreative power, an engulfing whirlpool in the great ocean!" ("Wem regt sich nicht . . . das Herz in hüpfender Lust, wenn ihm das innerste Leben der Natur in seiner ganzen Fülle in das Gemüt kommt! wenn dann jenes mächtige Gefühl, wofür die Sprache keine andere Namen als Liebe und Wollust hat, sich in ihm ausdehnt, wie ein gewaltiger, alles auflösender Dunst, und er bebend in süsser Angst in den dunkeln lockenden Schoss der Natur versinkt, die arme Persönlichkeit in den überschlagenden Wogen der Lust sich verzehrt, und nichts als ein Brennpunkt der unermesslichen Zeugungskraft, ein verschluckender Wirbel im grossen Ozean übrig bleibt!").

The theme of Novalis' symbolic novel, as it has survived in the fragment, is man's attempt to bring back the Golden Age when nature and man were one, a mystic union achieved only through love. To this theme all elements of the fragment have reference. In showing how this goal may be achieved, Novalis has set up, as it were, a scale of values. There are various levels to which man may attain or through which he may pass in seeking this goal. The highest level, before the final attainment of immortality through the recapture of the Golden Age, is the naive, intuitive feeling for nature possessed by artists and children. In next place we might rank the philosopher and naturalist, whose approaches, though sincere, are limited by their lack of feeling and their reliance upon reason. At the bottom of the scale, with the exception of those completely blind to nature, stands the "Scheidekünstler," the analytic scientist who sees only the parts and never the whole. In its claims for the superiority of irrational feeling over rational thought, its emphasis on individualism and its praise of poetry as man's closest link with nature, *Die Lehrlinge zu Sais* is one of the great documents of the Romantic spirit. While Novalis, as I have stated, presents the claims of philosophy and science sympathetically, he is careful to show their limitations. The strongest sympathies of the poet clearly lie with emotionalism and poetry.

The importance of imagery in *Die Lehrlinge zu Sais* can scarcely be overstated. In contrast to Novalis' early poetry, imagery as mere ornament is conspicuously absent. Imagery has now a variety of functions that must be understood if the poet's attitudes and meaning are to be appreciated. Metaphor, simile and personification—the three devices used most frequently—are employed to make palpable the ideas presented in the novel. In the letter to August Wilhelm Schlegel (IV, 229) in which Novalis expressed his intention to devote himself exclusively to poetry, he said also, "the sciences must all be made poetic" ("die Wissenschaften müssen alle poetisiert werden"). His intention becomes clear in *Die Lehrlinge zu Sais*. Instead of employing the abstract language of philosophy and the sciences, Novalis uses imagery even to present an account of these systems in palpable form. Terms such as "monad," "atom," "Neptunism," and "ideal" are deliberately avoided; instead, the ideas that these terms represent are incorporated in a literal image. Throughout the fragment imagery replaces direct identification. Again, an image often expands an idea previously advanced. The long personification image, which vividly renders the relationship of poet and scientist to nature, follows the statement that nature is best understood as a human being. Invariably, such an image is more persuasive than explicit statement. At the same time, the type of imagery employed by a speaker is a revelation of character. The naive nature of the apprentice is exposed by his almost exclusive use of literal images to express his thoughts, whereas the highly imaginative, figurative images employed by the handsome youth display his emotional nature and intuitive grasp of the great sympathy in nature. It is in the words of this young poet, particularly, that Novalis seeks, through imagery, to break the bonds of conventional language. The images of flame, fluid and vapor used by the youth are an attempt to express the inexpressible, to convey emotions which can be captured only in poetic imagery. Throughout the fragment the abstract and the unidentifiable are made concrete through imagery. Light images—fire, flame, stars, color—are used to reveal inner sympathies, the understanding of some idea, or the inner quality of an object and the quality it represents. The reverence of the teacher and the apprentices for nature is expressed concretely through their reverence for stones and plants. The order of nature is revealed through music images, and the outer manifestations of nature's spirit are represented metaphorically as the symbols of a language through which its meaning is expressed. The poet's metaphor makes of nature a living, dynamic, and sympathetic creature intelligible only through analogy with man's emotions.

Once created, a broad image is again evoked by a reference to the same area from which the image was taken, so that there evolves an image pattern. In the apprentice's mind the teacher's creative acts are linked to the creative forces in nature by music imagery, and the song of the clumsy apprentice, on his discovery of the wonderful stone, informs the teacher before the apprentice's return that the apprentice has discovered for himself the harmony of nature. This cross-reference within the imagery of the fragment, however, is of particular importance in the case of the two thematic images—the veil image and the spiral image. Through their recurrence and their function of linking action at two different levels—in the "Märchen" and in the larger work—these images assume symbolic character. The veil image, which occurs, explicitly and implicitly, four times in the fragment, expresses in symbol the theme of the novel. The spiral image is the symbol of the novel's action. Explicit reference is made to it in the words "Thus I too will describe my figure," and in the teacher's claim that all roads lead back to the temple. It underlies, as we have seen, the action of the fairy tale, and it is the pattern on which the first chapter is constructed. The chapter opens with the statement of the problem of the work and we return to this point, but on a higher plane, at the close of the chapter when the theme is expressed in symbol. The appreciation of the complementing function of the imagery is vital to our understanding of the author's purpose.

In *Die Lehrlinge zu Sais* Novalis' language has become the "Tropen- und Rätselsprache" to which reference was made in the first chapter of this study. It is, as was suggested at that point, a "language of enigma" to those hostile to poetry, to those who are not able to grasp the truths that poetic language can reveal. Implicit statement, through imagery, has become Novalis' preferred mode of communication with those to whom he wishes to impart his view of man's situation. This tendency, the most pronounced stylistic characteristic of Novalis, is established with the writing of *Die Lehrlinge zu Sais*. It is best exemplified at this point in the poet's use of the imagery of his "Märchen" to present the action of the larger work at a different level. This subtle method of providing the reader with a key to the meaning of the imagery of the greater context is, again, developed in the fables of Novalis' more ambitious prose work, *Heinrich von Ofterdingen*. Thus, with the creation of *Die Lehrlinge zu Sais*, Novalis has developed both a personal mode of presentation and a private system of symbols. In our analysis of his other major works we shall see the further growth of the poet's language of imagery. In these works Novalis persists in his concern for the problem of man's relationship to nature. Yet at the same time this immediate problem is seen as but one element of the supreme question of existence—that of man and his relationship to God and Christ.

CHAPTER IV

HYMNEN AN DIE NACHT

During approximately the same period in which the two chapters of *Die Lehrlinge zu Sais* were written Novalis composed his greatest work, the *Hymnen an die Nacht*. This cycle of six hymns in a mixture of rhythmic prose and verse, rich in boldly imaginative metaphor, is the most intensely subjective and lyric of his creations. Here the poet depicts the revelation that persuaded him of the truths of the Christian faith and sings of the joy of mystic experience. This, the best known of Novalis' works, was his only poetry to reach the public during his lifetime. It appeared in 1800 in the third volume of *Das Athenäum* after the original manuscript had been subjected to considerable revision. In this manuscript version, which dates from the autumn of 1799, the hymns are written more extensively in verse. The relative merits of the two versions has been the subject of much discussion.[1] Since comparison of them, however, shows that the revisions undertaken before publication were made by the author himself, we must accept the *Athenäum* version as the final form of the cycle and consider the manuscript version as but an intermediary stage of composition. It is to the *Athenäum* text, therefore, that this study is directed.

The hymns to the night present more difficulties of interpretation than does Novalis' other poetry. Critics have held frequently differing opinions both on the meaning of the work as a whole and

---

[1] Heinz Ritter, *Novalis' Hymnen an die Nacht* (Heidelberg, 1930), p. 94, argues that the *Athenäum* version is generally inferior and his interpretation of the hymns, therefore, is based largely on the manuscript text. Both Hiebel, pp. 172ff, and Max Kommerell, "Novalis: Hymnen an die Nacht," *Gedicht und Gedanke,* ed. H. O. Burger (Halle, 1942), pp. 202-236, use the manuscript version to a great extent in their interpretations.

on individual themes within the cycle. All too frequently quotations from Novalis' aphorisms and his other poetry have been introduced as aids to interpretation. Some critics have looked for the influence of contemporary philosophy, while others have tended to over-emphasize autobiographical elements, as a result of which their interpretation has depended extensively on the drawing of parallels between the hymns and the poet's letters and diaries. The dangers of these critical methods are obvious. The work itself is sub-ordinated to a discussion of the poet's life and his philosophic interests. If the hymns have meaning, this meaning should be found within the hymns themselves. It is my conviction that the cycle can be interpreted, using the imagery of the work as the basis of our approach, without reference to external elements.

The *Hymnen an die Nacht* depict, first, in esoteric imagery the revelation to Novalis of the true nature of night and its meaning for his existence. From this grows his understanding of Christianity as a religion of "night" and the meaning for mankind of the revel-ation through Christ of the true nature of death. Thus a unique personal experience assumes universal significance and symbolic character for Novalis. The growth of personal revelation into cosmic revelation is depicted in the hymns through the growth into symbols of the images created by the poet in the first hymn of the cycle. What difficulties there are in the hymns and what at first may appear to be contradictions can, I believe, be fully explained in light of the expansion of the area of reference embraced by these images and through the complementary function of the imagery of the cycle. It is, in fact, the cross reference of the imagery and the gradual growth of the images into symbols linking different spheres of reference that, more than anything else, give the work the character of a cycle. In my analysis of the individual hymns I shall show how the dominant images of the first hymn—the images of light and night, the grave, the vision and the figure of the poet's beloved, which have reference there only to the immediate experience depicted by the poet—are amplified and expanded in the succeeding hymns until finally they have universal reference.

The first hymn depicts the revelation to the poet of the true nature of night and his resultant understanding of the relationship between light and night. Content and form of this hymn go hand in hand, each stanza depicting a stage in the poet's initiation into the secrets of night. Remarkably, the cycle begins with the praise of light. In the first stanza an image of light is invoked, "light, which makes all creatures rejoice" ("das allerfreuliche Licht"). The image embraces all manifestations of light—"with its colors, its beams and waves; its gentle omnipresence as wakening day" ("mit seinen Farben, seinen Strahlen und Wogen; seiner milden All-gegenwart, als weckender Tag")—and it is at once expanded through simile and metaphor to represent light as the life force of the universe. Light is "breathed" by stars, stones, plants, and animals.[2] The enormous vitality of the earthly realm is emphasized by the poet's metaphor: "the contemplative, sucking plant and the wild, burning animal of many forms . . ." ("die sinnige, saugende Pflanze, und das wilde, brennende, vielgestaltcte Tier . . ."). Above all, light is the source of life for man, "the noble stranger" ("der herrliche Fremdling"), an epithet which suggests that man, though dependent on light for his life, is nevertheless not at home in the realm of light. In the dominant light image of the cycle Novalis now likens light to a king of all physical forces: "Like a king of nature's earthly realm it summons every force to countless transformations, forms and dissolves endless alliances, drapes its divine image about every creature of earth. Its presence alone reveals the wondrous splendor of the world's realms" ("Wie ein König der irdischen Natur ruft es jede Kraft zu zahllosen Verwandlungen, knüpft und löst unendliche Bündnisse, hängt sein himmlisches Bild jedem irdischen Wesen um.—Seine Gegenwart allein offenbart die Wunderherrlichkeit der Reiche der Welt"). Just as the authority of the monarch is invested in his subjects through the bestowing of a royal Order, so light makes all things on earth visible through its manifestation in them. To this image of light as a king, as a demanding power ruling the physical universe, almost all later light images have reference. The realm of King Light is a clearly defined

---

[2] Novalis may have been influenced in the shaping of this image by Lavoisier's theories of the process of combustion.

secular realm. It is the realm of visible objects, vital forces, and
the life of earth.

The second stanza shows the poet turning away from the realm
of light, despite its splendor and its wonders: "I turn aside to the
sacred, ineffable, mysterious night" ("Abwärts wend ich mich zu
der heiligen, unaussprechlichen, geheimnisvollen Nacht"). Yet,
despite the epithets Novalis employs to characterize the nature of
night (its spiritual and inexpressible qualities contrast vividly with
the attributes of the realm of light), he sings to night no song of
praise such as he had sung for light. Although he senses intuitively
some of night's qualities, he does not at this point understand
night's true nature. He is occupied with his own grief and despair,
made palpable through the images of the grave and isolation
through which they are expressed: "Far away lies the world, sunk
down into a deep grave, desolate and lonely is its place. In the
strings of my breast stirs the breath of profound grief" ("Fernab
liegt die Welt—in eine tiefe Gruft versenkt—wüst und einsam ist
ihre Stelle. In den Saiten der Brust weht tiefe Wehmut"). Like
an instrument sensitive to the wind (an allusion to the Aeolian
harp), the poet is stirred by his grief to long for death, as though
he would dissolve into tears and be mixed with the dew and with
the ashes of the body that lies in the grave: "I will sink down in
drops of dew and mingle with the ashes" ("In Tautropfen will ich
hinuntersinken und mit der Asche mich vermischen"). Memories
of his past happiness and youthful dreams pass before him "in
grey robes" (a ghostly image that evolves from the image of the
grave), but he finds no solace in night. Thus his thoughts turn
back again to light: "In other realms light pitched its gay pavilions"
("In andern Räumen schlug die lustigen Gezelte das Licht auf"),
an image suggesting the tents of a high-spirited, conquering army
led by a victorious King Light. Yet it is other realms, not that of
night, that light has conquered, and Novalis, still thinking of himself as a child of light, awaits anxiously the return of day.

Then a *sudden* revelation makes known to the poet the true
nature of night and rids him of his sadness. (The phrase "auf einmal" in the first sentence of this stanza clearly marks this turning
point in the hymn.) His question—"Do we find favor in your
eyes, too, dark night?" ("Hast du auch ein Gefallen an uns, dunkle
Nacht?")—reveals his surprise at his discovery that night, too, can

be apprehended as a living being, sympathetic to mankind. Beneath the cloak of night (Novalis had not before penetrated beyond this outer garment), there is a powerful intoxicating force—symbolized by the poppies night holds in her hands in this image—that brings comfort to him: "You raise the heavy pinions of my spirit" ("Die schweren Flügel des Gemüts hebst du empor"). His vision reveals to him the face of night: "with a glad start an earnest face I see, gently and devoutly bending over me and revealing beneath locks of hair endlessly intertwined a mother's precious youthfulness" ("ein ernstes Antlitz seh ich froh erschrocken, das sanft und andachtsvoll sich zu mir neigt, und unter unendlich verschlungenen Locken der Mutter liebe Jugend zeigt"). The Medusa-like head, the aspect of night that had previously caused the poet to turn back to light, displays now a face that is familiar, youthful and loving. It is this duality that makes Novalis "froh erschrocken." With the revelation of night's true nature, light now seems "poor and childish," its departure welcome. The poet realizes the reason for the hostility of light to night: "Only, then, because night lures your servants from you did you sow the radiant orbs in the far reaches of space, to proclaim your omnipotence, your return, in the periods of your withdrawal" ("Also nur darum, weil die Nacht dir abwendig macht die Dienenden, sätest du in des Raumes Weiten die leuchtenden Kugeln, zu verkünden deine Allmacht— deine Wiederkehr—in den Zeiten der Entfernung"). It is because night threatens the power of King Light that light has created the stars as viceroy-like symbols of its omnipotence and as a promise of its return. Yet, for Novalis, more divine than these symbols of light are the "eyes" opened within him by night. This night-sense is not dependent on light (that is, it is a spiritual, not a physical power), and it penetrates depths which light cannot reach, "the depths of a loving spirit" ("die Tiefen eines liebenden Gemüts").

Complementing the image of light as king of earth, Novalis creates an image of night as queen of the universe. It is to her that he now sings his praises. She, the "Weltkönigin," "prophetess of sacred realms" and the "guardian of sweet love," sends the poet's beloved to him. His beloved, "gentle loved one, lovely sun of night" ("zarte Geliebte—liebliche Sonne der Nacht"), becomes, as this last image suggests, the poet's link between the two realms of light and night. In the assurance that this link exists, Novalis can awaken from his vision to face life in the realm of light: "now I wake—for I am yours and mine" ("nun wach ich—denn ich bin dein und mein"). It is his beloved, Novalis says, who has initiated him into the new life of night ("du hast die Nacht mir zum Leben verkündet"), and at the same time has made him a man, one capable, that is, of facing the realities of existence in the realm of light. The hymn closes with the poet's fervent longing for mystic union with his beloved, expressed in boldly erotic imagery that suggests the vaporous commingling of the lovers in an eternity of passionate embrace: "consume my body with spectral fire so that I may mingle as air more fervently with you, and then forever will last our nuptial night" ("zehre mit Geisterglut meinen Leib, dass ich luftig mit dir inniger mich mische und dann ewig die Brautnacht währt").

The three stages of the poet's initiation into the secrets of night's meaning are thus portrayed through the imagery of the three stanzas of this hymn, as all the vital images of the cycle are created. Novalis depicts two realms, at first apparently irreconcilable and mutually exclusive. The realm of light is first praised in imagery of striking color and brilliance as the familiar realm of earth, of vital forces and visible splendor. Yet, because he senses that it is not the real home of man, the poet turns away to night. Initially he finds in night only a mirror of his own despairing grief, though he feels intuitively the spiritual qualities that attract man to night. It is a vision that reveals the true nature of night's realm, a realm of solace, youthfulness and love—essentially feminine qualities in contrast to the virile qualities of the realm of light. The two realms are linked by love, in the figure of the poet's beloved, and it is through love that night reaches into the realm of light. Night, the queen of love, is also the queen of the dead, since the poet's loved one is dead—a fact that is hinted at in the poet's longing for death and made clear in the final lines of the hymn. The grave of which Novalis speaks is the grave of his beloved, and it is his world that has been lowered into the grave with her body. But it is from the grave that his vision comes, a vision that shows him love does not end at the grave. This revelation enables him to bear the trials of life in the realm of light. He has found a new life in night's spiritual realm, the realm of love, a life that begins at the grave.

THE SECOND HYMN

With the assurance given him by his vision, Novalis indicated in the first hymn, he could awaken to face life in the realm of light. The second hymn shows him fully awake to the demands of earthly existence and aware of light's hostility to night and love: "Must the dawn again and again return? Does earth's power never end? Accursed activity consumes the divine efflorescence of night" ("Muss immer der Morgen wiederkommen? Endet nie des Irdischen Gewalt? unselige Geschäftigkeit verzehrt den himmlischen Anflug der Nacht"). Yet this hymn is, in fact, a song praising night's power over light, as the night image is expanded to embrace sleep. The relationship of sleep to night is subtly conveyed by allusion to "sacred sleep" ("Heiliger Schlaf"), the epithet binding sleep to night as a manifestation of the divine. Light is again depicted as a demanding power, calling men to its service and summoning the worshiper of night and love back to light's realm. The spiritual quality of night and love, on the other hand, is emphasized by an image of religious rites practiced by the lover: "Will love's secret sacrifice never burn eternally?" ("Wird nie der Liebe geheimes Opfer ewig brennen?"). However, the poet's question —"Must the dawn again and again return?"—is not one of resigned despair. He knows now that the power of light is limited, while that of Queen Night is boundless: "To light was allotted its span of time, but night's dominion knows neither time nor space" ("Zugemessen ward dem Lichte seine Zeit; aber zeitlos und raumlos ist der Nacht Herrschaft"). Limitless, too, is night's manifestation in sleep—not sleep as it exists in the imagination of the uninitiated: "Only fools fail to recognize you; they know sleep only as that shadow which you cast over us sympathetically in that twilight of the true night" [3] ("Nur die Toren verkennen dich und wissen von keinem Schlafe, als dem Schatten, den du in jener Dämmerung der wahrhaften Nacht mitleidig auf uns wirfst")— but the sleep that is the comforting manifestation of night's power on earth, felt by Novalis in wine, in the drug of almond oil and the poppy, and equated by him with erotic love: "They [the fools] do

---

[3] This example of catachresis—sleep metaphorically represented as a blanket—succinctly expresses the power of those possessed of the poet's "night sense" to recognize the metaphorical nature of all about them.

not know that it is you who hover about the bosom of the fair maid and make a heaven of her womb" ("Sie [die Toren] wissen nicht, dass du es bist der des zarten Mädchens Busen umschwebt und zum Himmel den Schoss macht"). Like the traditional image of sleep as the messenger of the gods in ancient legends, the final image of the hymn suggests, the sleep that Novalis praises is night's ambassador in the realm of light, an intoxicating inspiration that brings to the worshipers of Queen Night solace and assurance, though they must serve an alien king.

Thus the knowledge of which the poet boasts in this second hymn grows from the vision depicted in the first. This is one meaning of the revelation for his existence—the knowledge that, in the midst of life in the realm of light, the initiated can know the inspiration of night.

THE THIRD HYMN

The language and style of the third hymn differ markedly from the figurative language and mode of expression of the first and second hymns. Whereas Novalis employed before the present tense and direct forms of address, here he uses past tenses and indirect references. The poet here looks back on the nature and circumstance of his vision, reducing it to the level of unique personal experience. Much that was presented in the first hymn in figurative imagery is here recounted largely in literal images—contrast, for example, the earlier description of his grief: "In the strings of my breast stirs the breath of profound grief . . . The heavy pinions of my spirit . . ." with the third hymn's "Once when I shed bitter tears, when my hope drained away, dissolved in pain . . ." ("Einst da ich bittre Tränen vergoss, da in Schmerz aufgelöst meine Hoffnung zerrann . . ."). To understand the position of this hymn in the cycle and why Novalis gives such a literal account of his experience at the grave of his beloved after presenting it in metaphor in the first hymn, we must look ahead to the fourth, in which the poet shows how his personal revelation assumes universal significance. The growth of the one into the other is made more vivid through the juxtaposition of the third and fourth hymns. Further, the elements of Novalis' experience that assume particular significance in the fourth hymn are embodied in the dominant images of the third—the grave, the vision and the beloved. The third hymn is, as it were, a loving backward glance at the incident that so changed his own life before the fourth hymn reveals the universal significance of his experience.

In a series of literal images Novalis describes his grief as he stood at the grave of his beloved, and then the advent of night that broke the fetters binding him to the life of earth: "and suddenly the bonds of birth—the fetters of light—were rent" ("und mit einemmale riss das Band der Geburt—des Lichtes Fessel"). (The metaphorical bonds and fetters, which return later in the cycle, suggest that man is a prisoner in the realm of light, rather than a willing subject.) His sorrows fled as sleep—the inspired sleep of the second hymn—came over him: "you, night's inspiration, slumber of heaven, stole over me" ("du Nachtbegeisterung, Schlummer des Himmels kamst über mich"), bringing a vision of his beloved across the grave: "the landscape gently lifted; above the landscape floated my delivered, new-born spirit. The grave was turned into a cloud of dust—through the cloud I saw the transfigured features of my beloved" ("die Gegend hob sich sacht empor; über der Gegend schwebte mein entbundner, neugeborner Geist. Zur Staubwolke wurde der Hügel—durch die Wolke sah ich die verklärten Züge der Geliebten"). As he embraced her, the power of light and time was broken—"Thousands of years moved off into the distance like thunder clouds" ("Jahrtausende zogen abwärts in die Ferne, wie Ungewitter")—and their tears became a bond between them which, unlike the fetters that had bound him to the earth, was unbreakable. This dream-vision—"the first and only dream" ("der erste, einzige Traum")—Novalis states, inspired his faith in the "heaven of night" and in the light of that heaven, his beloved.[4]

THE FOURTH HYMN

After the third hymn has recalled the turning point in his existence, Novalis resumes his account of his deepening understanding of the relationship between light and night, taking up this theme again from the second hymn. That hymn had begun with the question, "Must the dawn again and again return?" and had gone

---

[4] This image is a variant of the first hymn's "gentle loved one, lovely sun of night."

on to show how the power of light is inferior to that of night. Now, in the fourth hymn, the poet foresees the dawn of eternity as the union of the two realms: "Now I know when the last dawn will be —when light no longer drives away night and love" ("Nun weiss ich, wenn der letzte Morgen sein wird—wenn das Licht nicht mehr die Nacht und die Liebe scheucht"). Then eternity will be an everlasting slumber—and here the word "slumber" has the implicit meaning of the eternal "nuptial night" of the first hymn and the "sleep" of the second, an eternal, intoxicating, erotic passion. Then his vision will become reality, "one inexhaustible dream" ("ein unerschöpflicher Traum"). His anticipatory longing for this state is expressed through an image complementing the image of this eternal sleep—"I feel within me a heavenly weariness" ("Himm- lische Müdigkeit fühl ich in mir")—and he shows in metaphor the meaning that the grave has acquired for him: "The pilgrimage to the holy grave was long and wearying, the cross burdensome" ("Weit und ermüdend ward mir die Wallfahrt zum heiligen Grab, erdrückend das Kreuz"). The road to the grave was an arduous one, for it was the death of his loved one that had led him there, but the grave became sacred as the source of his revelation. The cross on the grave, like the cross borne by Christ on the way to Golgotha, was burdensome to him, but now cross and grave have new meaning. From the grave there flows a rejuvenating flood, a wellspring of new life pure and bright but discernible only to those initiated into night's secrets: "The crystal wave, imperceptible to our ordinary senses, swells in the mound's dark womb . . ." ("Die kristallne Woge, die gemeinen Sinnen unvernehmlich, in des Hügels dunkelm Schoss quillt . . ."). In metaphor again, Novalis shows the universal significance of the grave, the bulwark denoting the bounds of King Light's powers. The grave is like a dike holding the sea of light in check, a dike "at the foot of which earth's tide breaks," and it is also the "frontier mountains of the world" from which men may look across, as the poet did in his vision, into the new realm, "night's dwelling place." Having experienced this revelation, man will never turn back willingly to the disquietude of the life of earth, "the land where dwells the light in eternal unrest" ("das Land, wo das Licht in ewiger Unruh hauset"). Instead, the grave will become a haven of peace, where, hermit-like, man will worship and love (again the two are equated), awaiting the hour of death, "the most welcome of all hours" ("die willkommenste aller Stunden"). In striking and esoteric metaphor developed from the earlier image of the life-giving flood that pours from the grave Novalis depicts the moment of death and the transfiguration that leads to eternal life. In death man is drawn down into the wellspring of life, his mortal parts floating to the surface to be carried away by storms, while his soul—"that which was sanctified by the touch of love" ("was heilig durch der Liebe Berührung ward")—is dissolved and flows along concealed courses into the realm beyond, where, like vapor, it mixes with other souls in mystic union. This forceful image suggests a process of purification. The final vapor metaphor, recalling the first hymn's allusion to a vaporous commingling in mystic union, clearly represents for the poet the ultimate stage in purification of the individual. Water and erotic images are joined in this metaphor, one of the most striking examples of Novalis' ability to bring together imagery from various areas of reference.

Once again, however, Novalis shows that the demands of earthly existence must be met by the worshiper of night, that light has power over man so long as he remains on earth. Light calls him back to its service, but his revelation has given him a more profound understanding and appreciation of the positive values of earthly existence and the physical universe—the brilliance and splendor of earth, the ordered harmony of the universe: "Gladly will I stir my sedulous hands, look about everywhere you need me —praise the full glory of your splendor—assiduously trace the beautiful fabric of your intricate creation—gladly observe the ingenious workings of your mighty radiant clock—fathom the harmony of forces and the laws of the miraculous workings of countless expanses and their periods" ("Gern will ich die fleissigen Hände rühren, überall umschaun, wo du mich brauchst—rühmen deines Glanzes volle Pracht—unverdrossen verfolgen deines künstlichen Werks schönen Zusammenhang—gern betrachten deiner gewaltigen, leuchtenden Uhr sinnvollen Gang—ergründen der Kräfte Ebenmass und die Regeln des Wunderspiels unzähliger Räume und ihrer Zeiten"). Yet, though his hands may serve King Light, his soul will worship night, the grave—"memory's moss-grown monument" ("der Erinnerung moosiges Denkmal")—and night's daughter, love. It is to love, particularly, that light is hostile, and the poet challenges light to show him love and beauty that can equal the love and beauty revealed to him by night in the person of his beloved: "Can you show me a heart eternally true? Has your sun friendly eyes that recognize me? Do your stars grasp my reaching hand? Return my gentle pressure and my caressing word?" ("Kannst du mir zeigen ein ewig treues Herz? Hat deine Sonne freundliche Augen, die mich erkennen? Fassen deine Sterne meine verlangende Hand? Geben mir wieder den zärtlichen Druck und das kosende Wort?"). Carried away by his emotion, Novalis asks whether light gave color and beauty to his beloved in her life on earth, or whether it was she who gave light greater meaning: "Did you adorn her with colors and light outline—or was it she who gave to your adornment more noble, more endearing import?" ("Hast du mit Farben und leichtem Umriss Sie geziert—oder war Sie es, die deinem Schmuck höhere, liebere Bedeutung gab?"). The realm of light has no joys to balance the delights of death. Everything, Novalis passionately asserts, that inspires man bears "night's hue" ("die Farbe der Nacht"). In this faith he proclaims that light owes its existence to night that gives it birth as a mother gives birth to her child. The poet, as a child of night, can claim that he existed before the world of light, for night, the mother of love and light, is also the mother of men who sent them into the world "to sanctify it through love that it might become a monument eternally contemplated—to plant it with unfading flowers" [5] (". . . sie zu heiligen mit Liebe, dass sie ein ewig angeschautes Denkmal werde—zu bepflanzen sie mit unverwelklichen Blumen"). However, Novalis realizes that this goal has not yet been attained— "Still the signs of our revelation are few" ("Noch sind der Spuren

---

[5] The flowers would seem to symbolize spiritual values that are foreign growths in the realm of light. Similar metaphor at other points in Novalis' works, particularly in *Heinrich von Ofterdingen*, suggests that this became a fixed symbol in the poet's mind. *Cf.* also the following entry in his diary (IV, 403): "There are so many flowers in this world that are of supernatural origin, flowers which do not prosper in this clime and which are actually heralds, messengers crying of a better existence. Among these flowers belong primarily religion and love" ("Es gibt so manche Blumen auf dieser Welt, die überirdischen Ursprungs sind, die in diesem Klima nicht gedeihen und eigentlich Herolde, rufende Boten eines besseren Daseins sind. Unter diese Blumen gehören vorzüglich Religion und Liebe"). The entry was made after the completion of the *Hymnen*.

unserer Offenbarung wenig")—but he foresees the future union of
light and night when time will end and light will die. Despite the
apparent irreconcilability of life and death, symbolized in the
hymn as the Titan-like resistance of light to the "old heaven,"
Novalis proclaims his faith in the attainment of this final union.
The cross, like the grave a symbol of death, has become for him
and for all initiated into night's secrets the symbol of a new life,
a symbol that—as the adjective "unverbrennlich" clearly indicates
here—light cannot destroy: "The cross stands unburnable, a flag
of victory for our kind" ("Unverbrennlich steht das Kreuz—eine
Siegesfahne unsers Geschlechts"). No longer "burdensome," the
cross is the symbol of the victory of night over light, of a new
life-in-death over the life of earth.

The final stanza of the hymn is a song of longing anticipation,
its erotic imagery recalling the poet's allusion in the first hymn to
an eternal nuptial night. Every pain will be a thorn of delight for
the singer as he "flows across" [6] into eternity. Freed from earth's
fetters, he will lie intoxicated in the womb of love. He imagines
himself standing in the realm of night, looking down on King Light
whose power ends at the grave: "I gaze from above/Down upon
you./At that mound/Your radiance vanishes" ("Ich schaue von
oben/Herunter nach dir./An jenem Hügel/Verlischt dein Glanz").
Death, "a shadow," brings the "cooling wreath," the symbol of
both victory and relief after the pain of earthly existence. Then,
in bold imagery and with great emotional emphasis, the poet calls
on Christ to draw him to Him: "Oh, Beloved!/Draw upon me
mightily/That I may fall asleep/And love" [7] ("O! sauge, Geliebter,
/Gewaltig mich an,/Dass ich entschlummern/Und lieben kann").
The drastic image, "O! sauge, Geliebter,/Gewaltig mich an,"
suggesting a vampire-like consuming of the lover by the beloved,
echoes earlier images of erotic ravishment, while death and erotic
love are now fully equated. It is, quite clearly, Christ whom
Novalis here addresses as "Geliebter," and this turning point in
the cycle is carefully anticipated in the imagery of this hymn. The

[6] This image springs from the earlier fluid images in which Novalis
depicts death and transfiguration. See above, p. 62.

[7] It is possible that Novalis is here using "sauge mich an" in the sense
of "suckle me," or in the sense of "draw me up," an image which, it has
been suggested to me, may be derived from mine workings.

cross is traditionally the symbol of Christ, the symbol of victory for the Christian community, and the thorns and the wreath to which the poet alludes combine with the cross image to introduce the figure of Christ. Thus the image of the "Geliebte," the poet's beloved, becomes the "Geliebter," the symbol of universal love. Similarly, the erotic passion that unites lovers is identified with the mystic apprehension of Christ by the individual. Finally, in expectant anticipation of the delights of death, the poet proclaims his faith in his new existence: "By day I live/In courage and faith/ And at night I die/In holy fire" ("Ich lebe bei Tage/Voll Glauben und Mut/Und sterbe die Nächte/In heiliger Glut"). His life in the realm of light is one of preparation and anticipation, while his knowledge affords him foretaste of the delights of death through the experience of "night" in dreams, narcosis, intoxication, erotic love and moments of religious inspiration.

THE FIFTH HYMN

The fourth hymn, introducing the figure of Christ to the cycle, leads to the fifth, which portrays Christianity as a religion of night. The images of light and night grow into symbols, respectively, of secular and Christian religions, while personal revelation becomes cosmic revelation. Novalis has carefully drawn a parallel between his personal revelation and the revelation of Christianity presented in this hymn by returning to the triadic structural pattern of the first. The first hymn, as we have seen, began with the depiction of the realm of light, from which the poet turned away. There followed an intermediary stage, when, although recognizing that in the realm of light man is a stranger, the poet had not realized the true nature of night. Finally night's secrets were revealed to him by his dream-vision and, at the same time, he gained deeper understanding of the realm of light. In the same fashion, the fifth hymn shows how men turned away from a religion of "light," passing through a middle period of irreligious speculation, and then how, through Christ, the religion of "night" was revealed.

Thus the poet's metaphorical representation of the growth of man to knowledge of the divine begins with an image of a world in which light was worshiped, the ancient world before the birth of Christ. It is useless to seek points of historical reference in this image. Although Novalis obviously had Greece in mind in drawing this picture of the ancient world, his image is a composite picture of all secular religions. It is thus not enough to say merely that the image represents Greece, since the intended antithesis between the religions of light and night would not then be fully realized. This world was ruled by iron fate, when the gods dwelt amongst men on earth, and the Titans, ancestors of both gods and men, lay powerless beneath the earth. The insensibility of this ancient people towards the transcendent is suggested by the poet's metaphor: "A dark, heavy blindfold lay about their trembling souls— infinite was the earth" ("Eine dunkle, schwere Binde lag um ihre bange Seele—Unendlich war die Erde"). Theirs was a world filled with light—"Above the dawn's red mountains, in the ocean's sacred womb dwelt the sun, the all-inflaming, living light" ("Über des Morgens roten Bergen, in des Meeres heiligem Schoss wohnte die Sonne, das allzündende, lebendige Licht")—and all creatures worshiped this life-giving power. This realm of light was made beautiful and intelligible by myth: "An old giant bore the blessed world . . . rivers, trees, flowers and animals had human senses . . . a god in the grapes; a loving, motherly goddess growing up in full golden sheaves; the sacred ecstasy of love a sweet devotion to the most beautiful of goddesses" ("Ein alter Riese trug die selige Welt . . . Flüsse, Bäume, Blumen und Tiere hatten menschlichen Sinn . . . ein Gott in den Trauben—eine liebende, mütterliche Göttin, empor wachsend in vollen goldenen Garben—der Liebe heiliger Rausch ein süsser Dienst der schönsten Götterfrau"). Only one element of horror existed: "It was death cut short this joyous feast/With fear and pain and tears" ("Es war der Tod, der dieses Lustgelag/Mit Angst und Schmerz und Tränen unterbrach"). The terrifying, nightmarish aspect of death destroyed the happiness of this ancient people. Against it even their gods were powerless. Its omnipresence, its effect upon the lives of these worshipers of light is made vivid in the three stanzas of verse in which Novalis describes their fear. Even the bold imagination and intellectual flame of their poets failed to answer satisfactorily the problem of death, for, although these worshipers of light sought to make death less horrifying by depicting it as a youth who extinguished the light of life and with it all recollection of former bliss, what lay beyond death—"the eternal night"—remained an unsolved riddle. "Thus song was sung for [i.e., to assuage] their sad want" ("So sang das Lied dem traurigen Bedarfe").

The religion portrayed by Novalis as the religion of light is a secular religion which failed to answer the supreme question of existence—the problem of death and what lies beyond the grave. As a result of this failure, Novalis shows, this "old world" came to an end and men lost their faith in the myth that had given meaning to their lives. He portrays a middle period when men turned away from the religion of light but when they had not had revealed to them the religion of night. The beauty and bliss of the ancient world were destroyed with the shattering of the myth: "The garden of the young race withered; up into freer, desolate space strove mankind, growing and no longer childlike" ("Des jungen Geschlechts Lustgarten verwelkte—hinauf in den freieren, wüsten Raum strebten die unkindlichen, wachsenden Menschen"). The poetic spirit, the image suggests, disappeared with man's development of his intellectual powers and consequent loss of naïveté, a process which opened new realms to him though leading him from an Eden to an arid world of analytic thought. The gods vanished, and nature, that had lived and enjoyed intercourse with man through the myth, was imprisoned in mathematical and philosophic terms: "The arid cipher and the harsh measure bound her with an iron chain. Life's immeasurable flower crumbled into obscure words as though into dust and air" ("Mit eiserner Kette band sie die dürre Zahl und das strenge Mass. Wie in Staub und Lüfte zerfiel in dunkle Worte die unermessliche Blüte des Lebens"). Faith and phantasy, the divine powers that had given harmony and form to the ancient world, were gone, replaced by a spirit of rationalism that is symbolized by a cold north wind blowing over a frozen world. The soul of the world withdrew to await the birth of the new world. Light, no longer the symbol of the gods, fled to other planets. Night became the "womb of revelation" (a metaphorical representation of night used by both Schleiermacher and Hölderlin), and it was in night that the gods slept, awaiting the time when they could go forth in more splendid form into a changed world. (We must assume that Novalis imagines the old gods reappearing in the figure of Christ.)

This middle period, then, is characterized essentially by a complete absence of the religious and poetic spirits, as a time of intellectual speculation when man sought to apprehend the secrets of life and death through the sciences and philosophy. Cut off from intimate communion with nature and from a knowledge of the divine, mankind passed through the stage of ambivalence towards the realm of light that Novalis himself had experienced.

The new world, coming from the "womb of revelation," appeared in the person of Christ, "a son of the first virgin and mother, the infinite fruit of a mysterious embrace" ("ein Sohn der ersten Jungfrau und Mutter—Geheimnisvoller Umarmung unendliche Frucht"). In literal images and metaphors that parallel the Bible story, Novalis portrays Christ's birth, the coming of the wise men from the East, the growth of Christ into manhood and the spread of His gospel of love. About Him new life flourished like blossoming flowers,[8] while the divine inspiration of His words is suggested by the metaphor depicting them as "sparks of a divine spirit." But the first to recognize the true significance of Christ for mankind was a Greek poet, "ein Sänger," who gave his heart to Christ. In Christ the "singer" sees the torch-bearing youth of his own religion: "Thou art that youth who long has stood,/Sunk in thought, upon our graves . . . Thou art death and only in Thee shall we be made whole" ("Der Jüngling bist du, der seit langer Zeit/Auf unsern Gräbern steht in tiefem Sinnen . . . Du bist der Tod und machst uns erst gesund").

The figure of the singer has been the subject of much discussion. Attempts have been made to identify this Greek poet with the apostle Thomas, with John the Evangelist, and with other historical figures. It has even been suggested that it is Novalis himself. None of the interpretations hitherto advanced is completely convincing. The imagery, I believe, supplies a better explanation. The figure of the singer grows from the image of the ancient world, a world of myth, of myth created by poets. The Greek poet, symbolizing the creators of this myth, is the first to recognize the advent of

---

[8] The flowers again seem to be symbols of spiritual values. Runge, in a letter to Tieck, December 1, 1802, speaks of flowers as physical representations of God. See Philipp Otto Runge, *Schriften, Fragmente, Briefe,* ed. Ernst Forsthoff (Berlin, 1938), pp. 34f. Kommerell, pp. 231ff, takes Novalis' use of imagery here as the basis for his thesis that Novalis was seeking to create a new, poetic Christianity. I cannot see any justification for this interpretation, for Novalis in no way deviates from the tenets of the Christian tradition.

the new world in Christ. Thus Novalis shows that what poetry had previously failed to do—satisfactorily interpret the riddle of death—it now does through Christ. Likewise, it is Christ-inspired poetry, represented by the Greek poet carrying the gospel to Indostan, that links the worlds of East and West, as poetry, through Christ, links old world and new.

The Greek poet recognizes in Christ the true nature of death, the answer to the problem that his own religion had failed to answer; and Novalis goes on to show that it was in fact Christ's death that freed mankind from the death-horror of the old world and made death the door for mankind to a new life in eternity. Christ's death and resurrection, not His Advent, marked the hour of birth of the new world: "Accompanied by horrible fear the hour of birth of the new world approached. He struggled hard with the horrors of the old death, heavy lay upon Him the weight of the old world" ("In entsetzlicher Angst nahte die Stunde der Geburt der neuen Welt. Hart rang er mit des alten Todes Schrecken— Schwer lag der Druck der alten Welt auf ihm"). The continuing images suggest that Christ destroyed death in its old form and created, by His agony and sacrifice, a new death that is as tranquil as sleep: "then came the redeeming hand of eternal love and He fell asleep" ("da kam der ewigen Liebe lösende Hand—und er entschlief"). (Later, Novalis refers to Christ, as He lies in the tomb, as the "slumberer.") The stone at the entrance to His tomb is for Novalis symbolic of the stone on the grave of mankind, "the age-old stone," and with its removal the death-horror was ended. The transfigured Christ stepped forth into a transformed world. With His resurrection a new concept of life and death was created, metaphorically depicted by Christ's burial in His tomb of the body of the old world: "with His own hand [He] buried the old corpse in the abandoned cave and set over it with His almighty hand the stone no power may raise" ("begrub mit eigner Hand den alten Leichnam in die verlassene Höhle, und legte mit allmächtiger Hand den Stein, den keine Macht erhebt, darauf").

In this hymn Novalis is clearly taking issue with the intellectual heritage of German classicism, particularly with the belief that the pagan concept of death is beautiful, the Christian ugly. Novalis is at pains to show the inadequacy of the Greek world and its religion, though his picture of it is by no means entirely depreciatory. The image of the stone placed on the tomb containing the body of the old world—"the stone no power may raise"—suggests his belief that the Greek world can never be resurrected in its old form. The spirit that gave it life has been embraced by the spirit of the "new world" of Christianity.

The final prose passage of the hymn shows that Christ's death and resurrection have become the vision that has initiated mankind into the secrets of death, a vision that we may still see: "Thy beloved children, ... joyous in their alarm, still see Thee resurrected and themselves with Thee" ("deine Lieben ... sehn dich noch immer, freudig erschreckt, auferstehn—und sich mit dir").[9] Thousands have relived this experience and have followed Christ to rule with Him and the Virgin "in the realm of love ... in the temple of divine death" ("im Reich der Liebe ... im Tempel des himmlischen Todes"). For Novalis, drawing on his personal revelation of the nature of death, night and love, Christianity is a religion of night because it reveals the true nature of death as a source of new life in the eternal realm of love that lies beyond the grave; because, in contrast to the religion of light, it proclaims that death is not an end but a beginning. Just as the poet's beloved initiated him into the secrets of night, so Christ initiates mankind into the secrets of death.

The first hymn ended with the expression of the poet's longing for mystic union with his beloved after his revelation. In like manner, the fifth hymn ends with a communal song of desire for mystic union after the revelation of the meaning of death through Christ. Again the raising of the stone serves Novalis as an image of universal resurrection: "Raised up is the stone,/Resurrected is mankind./We all are Thine/And feel no fetters" ("Gehoben ist der Stein/Die Menschheit ist erstanden/Wir alle bleiben dein/Und fühlen keine Banden"). Freed of the fetters that had bound him to the earth (and, implicitly, to the despotism of King Light), the Christian may look forward to the final Communion and the end of grief. Death, no longer a horror, calls mankind to the "wedding" (an echo of the "Brautnacht" of the first hymn), that is both a *unio*

---

[9] It is most revealing to see the phrase "froh erschrocken" of the first hymn, by which the poet characterized his own vision of night, finding an echo in the words "freudig erschreckt." It is further evidence of the drawing of the parallel between the two revelations.

mystica and the union of the realms of light and night. It is interesting to see that, after the introduction of Christ to the cycle, Novalis draws more and more on Biblical images and on imagery hallowed by repeated use in the hymns of the Christian church. Now, as the image of the wedding is developed, he alludes to the parable of the wise and foolish virgins: "Brightly burn the lamps,/ The virgins are at hand./Of oil there is no need" ("Die Lampen brennen helle/Die Jungfraun sind zur Stelle/Um Öl ist keine Not"). Similarly, the singers' longing for the coming of Christ is expressed in an image that recalls the vision of St. John the Divine of a triumphant host with Christ at its head: "O that the distance would resound/Now with Thy approaching procession" ("Erklänge doch die Ferne/Von deinem Zuge schon"). Yet, juxtaposed to these images is an image that springs from Novalis' earlier metaphorical depiction of the union of the realms of earth and heaven: "And would that the stars might call to us/With human tongue and sound" ("Und ruften uns die Sterne/Mit Menschenzung' und Ton"). Traditional symbol and the imagery of the cycle are then joined in the person of the Virgin: "To Thee, Mary, are lifted/A thousand hearts" ("Nach dir, Maria, heben/Schon tausend Herzen sich"). Mary, a traditional symbol of the love of Heaven, becomes equated in the cycle with night, for Christ came, it was said, from the "womb of revelation," from night, the realm of love. It is to Mary that the Christians on earth turn for solace, longing to be united with Her and their loved ones in eternity. The grave is no longer a symbol of grief for mankind—"Now at no grave in pain shall weep/He who believes and loves" ("Nun weint an keinem Grabe,/Für Schmerz, wer liebend glaubt")—while night has become a source of inspiration and solace: "Night's inspiration comes/To soothe his longing" ("Die Sehnsucht ihm zu lindern,/ Begeistert ihn die Nacht"). Again eternity is foreseen as the union of the realms of light and night, depicted as the union of the stars with man. Then there will be one eternal night of bliss, in which God's countenance will be the light of all—an image recalling the poet's depiction of his beloved as the "sun of the night."

THE SIXTH HYMN

The final hymn of the cycle stands somewhat apart stylistically, being the only one written completely in verse. However, it is unquestionably linked to the other hymns by its theme and imagery. The sixth hymn, the song of the Christian community on earth and their praise of the life that awaits them in eternity, is essentially a postlude to the cycle after the climax of the fifth. The watchword of the singers is the title of this hymn, "Longing for Death" ("Sehnsucht nach dem Tode"), for they turn away from the realm of light and regard their suffering on earth as a sign that they will soon gain the realm for which they long: "Down into earth's womb,/Away from the realm of light./Raging pain and wild shock /Are signs of glad departure" ("Hinunter in der Erde Schoss,/Weg aus des Lichtes Reichen,/Der Schmerzen Wut und wilder Stoss/ Ist froher Abfahrt Zeichen"). Eternity is praised in the symbols of night and sleep, while day—the life of earth—is seen only as the preparation for the richer life after death: "Exhausted by day's hot labor/And withered by long grief,/The joy of this foreign clime is gone,/We will go home to our Father" ("Wohl hat der Tag uns warm gemacht,/Und welk der lange Kummer./Die Lust der Fremde ging uns aus,/Zum Vater wollen wir nach Haus"). (Here again we find Novalis employing a variant of an image used earlier in the cycle; in this case an echo of the image of the first hymn that depicted man as a "stranger" ("Fremdling") in the realm of light.) Life in the earthly realm is empty for the Christians, for the true faith, "the old" ("das Alte"), is disdained and other beliefs, "the new" ("das Neue"), seek to replace it. Thus the Christian, who looks back longingly to a former time, a "Vorzeit," when the true faith was manifest, is condemned to loneliness in a world where men fail to recognize the truth. This "Vorzeit" now serves the Christian as a symbol of living faith. In the fourth stanza it is depicted as a time when man had mystic knowledge of God and when saints dwelt among us, while the fifth cites the Children's Crusade as a symbol of the true faith. Again, the sixth stanza shows the "Vorzeit" as the time when God walked on earth among men in the person of Christ and sacrificed Himself for mankind. Now, however, the veil of night has been cast over it—we must, of course, infer that the light of the Enlightenment dominates the world of the singers—and the Christians see it only in symbol. The loved ones who have already passed to the world beyond call to those remaining behind—the longing for union exists in both realms,

The last stanza, envisioning the final mystic union, invokes again the bold erotic imagery in which Novalis invariably depicts the life after death, as Christ is identified as the bride, the beloved: "Hinunter zu der süssen Braut,/Zu Jesus, dem Geliebten." Twilight, the merging of light and night, symbolizes the union of heaven and earth: "Take comfort, dusk's grey light appears/To His children, the distressed./A dream will break our chains/And lower us into our Father's lap" ("Getrost, die Abenddämmerung graut/Den Liebenden, Betrübten./Ein Traum bricht unsre Banden los/Und senkt uns in des Vaters Schoss"). Novalis' own dream vision, "the first and only dream," had broken the fetters of light and linked him with his beloved across the grave. In the same way, he indicates, the final vision dreamed by everyone in the sleep of death, the vision that becomes reality, "one inexhaustible dream," will break the fetters that bind man to life on earth and unite him with God.

The cycle of hymns to the night, then, depicts the growth of personal revelation into universal revelation, the growth of the understanding of the true nature of night into the interpretation of Christianity as a revealed religion of night—a religion that proclaims death the beginning of life. Similarly, the cycle shows the extension of the discovery that human love can reach across the grave into the realization that God's love reaches into the world through Christ. From the first revelation that night was the poet's sphere of communion with his dead beloved springs the realization that death is the door to mystic union with Christ in Heaven. The growth of personal experience into knowledge of universal significance is portrayed through the expansion of the images created in the first hymn.

Having analyzed the imagery with reference to its immediate context, we may now demonstrate how each image is expanded throughout the cycle. When Novalis alludes in the final hymn to the "realm of light," the image governs an area of reference gradually defined throughout the cycle. The image is created in the first hymn; succeeding hymns make clear its limits, emphasize more and more those aspects of it that are repellent to those initiated into night's secrets, and show why poet and mankind must turn away from light's domain. The realm of light is the visible physical universe in which both man and love are foreign growths. Both the time of its existence and its powers are limited by night. The worship of light, a religion of this world, failed to satisfy man, as the fifth hymn shows, because it could not answer the problem of death. Life cannot reveal the true nature of death, and when the Christians, in the sixth hymn, turn away from the realm of light, their reason for so doing is implicit in the image. Light—the life of this world and its reason—has failed, despite its acknowledged brilliance and splendor, to give them what they sought.

The image of night is greatly expanded, until it finally embraces a broad area of reference. The realm of Queen Night is the spiritual realm, the realm of love, death and eternity. Night's infinite power reaches into the realm of light through love and through that intoxicating, erotic force the poet calls sleep. While light is the sustainer of life on earth, its own existence is sustained by night. Night is the giver of life, the eternal feminine force of the universe, the mother of men, of the dead, of love, even of light itself. Through the complementary nature of the imagery, night is eventually equated with Mary, the mother of love, the "womb of revelation," whence Christ came to bring to the world a new concept of life and death. It is to the night that gave them birth that men return in death. Thus in one symbol the poet and the Christian can praise the power that gave them life, that sustains them in life through love, that gives them the promise of a richer life after death, as well as the death which takes them into that new life that is eternal night.

The expansion of the other vital images—the grave, the beloved, and the dream-vision—parallels that of the night image. The grave is first the grave of the poet's beloved, the source of his vision, and it becomes the source of mankind's revelation. As the "frontier mountain range" of the world, it defines the limits of the power of light and at the same time it offers mankind a vision of the realm of night. At first the bridge across which the poet is re-united with his beloved, the grave becomes, through Christ's death and resurrection, the bridge across which mankind enters into heaven.

Love, the force that links the realms of light and night, is personified in the first hymn in the figure of the poet's beloved, and about this figure the remarkable erotic imagery of the cycle develops. The vision of an eternity of ravishing passion in union with his beloved is the poet's first glimpse of a life beyond the grave. Throughout the cycle similar erotic images evoke a picture of an eternal nuptial night. Thence the poet's beloved, "Geliebte," is boldly identified with Christ as the symbol of universal love, "Geliebter . . . süsse Braut," with whom the Christian longs to be united. Again, it is Christ who initiates mankind into the secrets of death just as the poet's beloved initiated him into the secrets of night. The poet's longing for mystic union with his beloved and with Christ is expressed through the same erotic metaphor. Divine and human love are equated through the expanding imagery, and eroticism becomes for Novalis a foretaste of the delights of Heaven—one aspect of religious experience.

The final important image is the dream-vision. When the poet says in the first hymn that he can awaken after his revelation, he reveals that his vision came to him in a dream, a fact made explicit by allusion in the third hymn to "the first and only dream," the vision dreamed in the "slumber of heaven." Like the grave image, this image assumes symbolic character when Novalis foresees eternity as the realization of the state revealed by the dream, "when slumber will be eternal and there will be only one inexhaustible dream." It is to this image that the poet returns at the close of the cycle when he says that a dream, the final dream dreamed in death, will break the fetters of life and lead man to God.

Thus the images grow throughout the cycle, linking each hymn with the next and giving the cycle its unity. The full meaning of each hymn is realized only with reference to the context of the work as a whole. Similarly, the individual images can be appreciated fully only if we examine their function as elements of the total presentation. It is impossible, for example, to grasp the area of reference embraced by the imagery of the sixth hymn unless the growth of the images in the cycle is understood. Again, when Novalis refers to himself in the fourth hymn as "the weary one," the metaphor has meaning only in the context of its reference to the image of sleep, the symbol of eternal eroticism and everlasting slumber of Heaven. Many of the minor images of the cycle owe their existence to their relationship to the major images examined above. Thus, the image of the cross and that of the stone draw their particular meaning from the expanded images of night, the beloved and the grave. The metaphorical fetters binding man to life on earth derive from the image of a despotic King Light. In all, then, we find integrated skillfully with the total presentation and often reinforced by epithet a pattern of imagery which gradually and as a whole reveals the poet's meaning and attitudes. More than in any other of his poetic works, Novalis turns to imagery in the *Hymnen an die Nacht* to express his emotions and beliefs. The boldness and drastic quality of many of the images, such as the erotic images and metaphors in which the poet depicts death and transfiguration, seem to represent Novalis' striving to present in palpable terms his unique experience of the nature of death and of the relationship of erotic love to religious inspiration. These images are even more striking when juxtaposed to traditional images drawn from Biblical sources and the metaphor of the Christian hymn. However, incongruity is avoided as the poet's own metaphor grows into universal and traditional symbol, as when, for example, the image of Queen Night is equated with Mary, the Queen of Heaven, through the fact that both are depicted in the hymns as the mother of love.

In this poignant representation of the poet's experience we have the supreme expression of that devotion to night allegedly characteristic of the German Romantics as a group. Yet it will be recognized that specific and personal qualities attach to "night" as the word is here used by Novalis. Characteristic of the general Romantic approach to night (if, indeed, one can speak of such an approach at all), is that of the despondent, isolated Novalis in the first hymn before his initiation into night's secrets: "I turn aside to the sacred, ineffable, mysterious night." It is through his vision that there comes to the poet the personal and unique knowledge of night of which he later sings. Yet it has been argued that the title given to the cycle is not a fitting one, that it cannot apply to the latter part of the work.[10] This objection is not to the

---

[10] Hiebel, p. 171.

word "Hymnen" in the title, but rather to the fact that the cycle is dedicated to the night. Such an objection can rest only on the failure to understand the development to which the image of night is subjected in the work. In developing this image into a symbol of the spiritual, the divine, and the feminine qualities of the universe, Novalis has created a symbol which must have had as universal a significance in his eyes as "das Ewig-Weibliche" had for Goethe. The night to which Novalis dedicates his impassioned outpouring is the night-symbol, with all the elements of reference this symbol embraces. It is to this symbolic character that Novalis points in his climactic utterance in the fourth hymn: "Does not everything that inspires us bear night's hue?"

CHAPTER V

GEISTLICHE LIEDER

The reader who proceeds from Novalis' *Hymnen an die Nacht* to his *Geistliche Lieder* cannot fail to be struck by the great difference in tone of the two works. The initial surprise at the dissimilarity of techniques employed by the poet is likely to be followed, however, by a sense of familiarity with the themes in the fifteen sacred songs. Here again we find Novalis giving poetic expression to his belief in the power of Christ to transform the existence of the individual and to reveal death as the source of new life. Here, too, we find Novalis equating human and divine love, praising eroticism as one aspect of religious experience, and singing of the joys of mystic apprehension of Christ. Indeed, the sacred songs would seem, like the hymns to the night, to owe their inspiration to the poet's experience at the grave of his fiancée, explicitly referred to in the fourth song when he praises the vision that revealed Christ to him. The occurrence of similar themes in the two cycles indicates that both were composed at approximately the same time, namely in the autumn of 1799, at the height of Novalis' religious fervor. With choice of theme, however, similarity virtually ends. The works differ markedly in mode of expression, in form, and in the nature of their presentation. In the *Hymnen* Novalis seems to seek to communicate only to the initiated his unique understanding of the secrets of night, death and love, creating, in a mixture of rhythmic prose and verse, a work that challenges the imaginative powers of the reader. In his sacred songs, however, Novalis turns to more traditional forms with conventional strophe and rhyme scheme. The contrast in the use of language is equally striking. The language of the hymns to the night is frequently obscure, ambiguous and rich in esoteric imagery. In the sacred songs the poet's language is simple, direct, and relatively free of such imagery. The images invoked by Novalis in the songs are generally traditional images that in many instances can be traced back to the Bible. It is rare that we meet with an image that strikes us as peculiarly Hardenbergian. Stylistically *Hymnen an die Nacht* and *Geistliche Lieder* stand far apart. The title which Novalis himself wished his sacred songs to bear, "Probe eines neuen, geistlichen Gesangbuchs," [1] would suggest that in them the poet was seeking to communicate with a vastly different audience, one familiar only with the conventions of the Christian hymn. The adoption of certain of these songs as hymns attests to Novalis' success in capturing the simple tone and naive spirit of the genre.

At first sight the songs of this group appear deceptively simple, each seemingly complete in itself and unrelated to the others. Yet if the individual songs are analyzed with reference to the larger context of the group, we discover that each is in fact an element of a cycle that has artistic balance and antithesis of theme. The full meaning of each song is realized only within this cyclic structure. Together the songs depict the total experience of Novalis' relationship to Christ, while the individual songs expand and amplify particular aspects of this relationship. As in the hymns to the night, the experience of the individual is projected against a cosmic background, as the poet's personal discovery of Christ is equated with the redemption of the world by the Saviour. Thus we find Novalis drawing an implicit parallel between his own despairing condition before his discovery of Christ and the hopeless state of the world before His coming, between the new life he has received from Christ's hands and the rejuvenation of the world through Christ's love. In all, the cycle portrays the growth in Christ of individual and mankind, from the uncertain fears of a life without Him, through the jubilant expectation of the Saviour's

---

[1] This "Sample of a New Book of Sacred Songs" was intended for *Das Athenäum*, but the complete group of songs was first published in the posthumous edition of Novalis' works in 1802. Seven of them had appeared earlier in the same year in *Der Musenalmanach*, some months after the poet's death. On both these occasions and in all subsequent editions the songs have borne the title "Geistliche Lieder." In his notes Novalis refers to "Christian songs" ("Christliche Lieder") (III, 319), but requests that they be published under the heading cited here (IV, 325). It is assumed that the name under which the songs are now known was chosen by either Friedrich Schlegel or Ludwig Tieck.

appearance, the joy at being freed from the fear of death, the lament at His death and the triumph of the Resurrection, to the revelation of the omnipresence of Christ's love and the calm, childlike assurance that accompanies this revelation. All these themes are introduced, overture-like, in the first song of the group, to be taken up and given fuller expression later in the cycle.

A study of the imagery of these songs effectively reveals the complex structure of the cycle, the inner relationship of the songs. The recurrence of certain images, the choice of metaphors from the same area of reference, and the development later in the cycle of images merely suggested in the first song give an inner unity to the cycle. This unifying function is an important aspect of the songs' imagery. More significant, perhaps, is that the individual images, conventional as these often are, reveal to the reader the nature of Novalis' religious experience and define the relationship of the poet to his Saviour. Indeed, the imagery reveals the character of Novalis' Christ.

In studying the imagery of the cycle we may best use the key Novalis has provided in the first song, taking up the various themes and images introduced there and seeing how these are re-echoed, modified and expanded throughout the cycle.

The first two stanzas of the opening song depict the state of the individual without Christ, an existence that the poet had known and which would still be his, had he not discovered the Saviour. This inner state of fear, uncertainty and hopelessness is revealed primarily through a series of literal images: "Destined to suffer fear and anguish,/I should stand alone in this vast world./I should not know for sure anything that I loved,/The future would be a dark abyss ... Alone, consumed by love and yearning,/Each day would seem to me as night;/I should follow only in hot tears/The wild course of life" ("Zu Furcht und Ängsten auserlesen,/Ständ' ich in weiter Welt allein./Nichts wüsst' ich sicher, was ich liebte,/Die Zukunft wär' ein dunkler Schlund ... Einsam verzehrt von Lieb' und Sehnen,/Erschien' mir nächtlich jeder Tag;/Ich folgte nur mit heissen Tränen/Dem wilden Lauf des Lebens nach"). The impossibility of such an existence is given its most outspoken form in the third song, the imagery of which echoes the lines quoted above and where the abyss image returns as the symbol of bottomless despair. This same image is found again in the eleventh song,

with the same function: "And will you not open your doors/To
Him who closed the abyss for you?" ("Und öffnet ihr nicht eure
Türen/Dem, der den Abgrund zu euch schlug?"). Similarly, we
find variants of the images of darkness, gloom and isolation
recurring whenever Novalis wishes to convey the nature of life
without Christ: "There are times so anxious,/Moods so gloomy,/
When everything is seen from afar/In ghost-like form ... And
deep nights weigh/Ponderously upon our souls ..." (X); "Our view
is limited by clouds/Through which breaks no ray of hope" (XIII)
("Es gibt so bange Zeiten,/Es gibt so trüben Mut,/Wo alles sich
von weiten/Gespenstisch zeigen tut ... Und tiefe Nächte decken/
Die Seele zentnerschwer ..." (X); "Wolken unsern Blick be-
schränken,/Die kein Hoffnungsstrahl durchblickt ..." [XIII]).

The transformation wrought in the individual by his acceptance
of Christ is depicted in the third and fourth stanzas. This change
is made particularly palpable by the use of imagery antithetical to
the earlier images of darkness and gloom: "How quickly a shining
life consumes/The bottomless darkness ... Destiny is made
radiant through Him" ("Wie schnell verzehrt ein lichtes Leben/
Die bodenlose Finsternis ... Das Schicksal wird verklärt durch
ihn"). These tones of joy reverberate in other songs, and the
images of light that consume darkness are employed to depict the
power of Christ to transform and rejuvenate. Thus in the second
song we find the approaching birth of Christ heralded by a brilliant
light that rejuvenates an age characterized by its drabness of color:
"Far in the East it is turning bright,/Grey days are finding youth;/
From the bright well of colors/A long deep draught" ("Fern im
Osten wird es helle,/Graue Zeiten werden jung;/Aus der lichten
Farbenquelle/Einen langen tiefen Trunk!"). This capacity of Christ
to change the life of those who know His love is portrayed with
forceful succinctness in the continuing images of the first song:
"And even in the North must India/Blossom happily about the
Loved One" [2] ("Und Indien muss selbst im Norden/Um den Ge-

---

[2] The image of the Polar region transformed into an exotic land, represented here by India, is one of Novalis' favorite metaphors—one of the
rare uses of nontraditional imagery in the cycle. It occurs implicitly in
the fifth hymn to the night, cf. above p. 67, and in Klingsohr's "Märchen."
There Arcturus' kingdom is first portrayed as the region of the North Pole.
The coming of a new Golden Age brings to it luxuriant growth.

liebten fröhlich blühn"). Elsewhere other growth images emphasize
this life-giving power: "Everywhere there springs from graves/New
life, new blood . . . [the Divinity] Has quickly awakened in south
and north/Seed buds of heaven" ("Überall entspringt aus Grüften/
Neues Leben, neues Blut . . . [die Gottheit] Hat im Süden und im
Norden/Himmelskeime rasch geweckt" [II]), and in the twelfth
song, when the poet declares his longing for a second coming of
Christ, metaphors from the same area of reference depict a world
anticipating new life with the appearance of the Saviour: "The
earth stirs, grows verdant, lives . . . The winter yields" ("Die Erde
regt sich, grünt und lebt . . . Der Winter weicht"). Related images
portraying the revitalization of the dead body reveal Christ as the
source of life for the individual metaphorically dead without Him:
"With Him comes new blood and life/Into your dead bones" (III);
"Every heart, spirit and mind/Will begin a new dance" (II) ("Mit
ihm kommt neues Blut und Leben/In dein erstorbenes Gebein"
(III); "Alle Herzen, Geister und die Sinnen/Werden einen neuen
Tanz beginnen" [II]).

   With the transformation of the individual, the first song goes on,
the world about him is also transformed: "Life becomes an hour
of love,/The whole world speaks love and joy" ("Das Leben wird
zur Liebesstunde,/Die ganze Welt spricht Lieb' und Lust"). The
recognition of the omnipresence of love is the high point of
revelation for the individual, and in the climactic seventh song,
"Hymne," Novalis proclaims love's inspiring and intoxicating
power. Here the love of Christ and sexual love are equated, as
manifestations of one cosmic force, in imagery reminiscent of that
of the hymns to the night. The symbols of this cosmic love are
the body and the blood—whether of Christ or of passionate lovers
ravished in their sexual hunger—transformed into symbols of the
divine. Few, Novalis asserts, know the secret of love and few
know the insatiable hunger and thirst of lovers. The divine significance of the sacrament is a riddle to earthly senses, but it can be
revealed through the inspiring power of erotic love: "But he who
at any time/From hot, beloved lips/Sucked the breath of life,/
Whose heart was melted into trembling waves by sacred fire,/
Whose eyes were opened/To the unfathomable depths/Of heaven,/
Such a one will eat of His body/And drink of His blood/Eternally"
("Aber wer jemals/Von heissen, geliebten Lippen/Atem des

Lebens sog,/Wem heilige Glut/In zitternde Wellen das Herz
schmolz,/Wem das Auge aufging,/Dass er des Himmels/Uner-
gründliche Tiefe mass,/Wird essen von seinem Leib/Und trinken
von seinem Blute/Ewiglich"). Who, the poet asks, can say that
he has guessed the significance of the earthly body or that he
understands the quality of blood? Yet, he goes on, in the act of
love the lovers are completely transformed into these divine
symbols: "One day everyone will be/One body,/In divine blood/
Will swim the blessed pair" ("Einst ist alles Leib,/E i n Leib,/In
himmlischem Blute/Schwimmt das selige Paar"), and he longs to
see the world so transformed: "O that the ocean/Would turn red/
And the rock swell up/In fragrant flesh!" ("O! dass das Weltmeer
/Schon errötete,/Und in duftiges Fleisch/Aufquölle der Fels!").
The imagery, embracing the act of Communion, suggests the
devouring of the beloved by the lover; the feast of love is never-
ending and desire only productive of greater desire, while the
object of love, "das Genossene," consumed by the impassioned
lover, is transformed: "What has been enjoyed is transformed/By
ever more tender lips/More fervently and more closely" ("Von
immer zärteren Lippen/Verwandelt wird das Genossene/Innig-
licher und näher"). This power of love to transform all is the
secret of love of which the poet spoke at the beginning of the song,
and this is the divine significance of the sacrament—the transformation of the host and the wine into the body and blood of Christ
through the power of His love. Through the dual nature of the
song's symbols divine and human love are equated. Both are part
of a cosmic force that, in the image of the first song, causes the
whole world to speak "love and joy." [3] Yet both human and
divine love can be comprehended only by direct experience, Novalis concludes in the seventh song; the relationship of the two is
grasped only by those who have felt their satiating power within:
"If the sober[4]/Had but once tasted,/They would abandon every-
thing/And would join us/At the table of longing/That is never
bare./They would recognize/Love's infinite wealth/And would

---

[3] "Joy" is here a translation of "Lust," a word which like "Wollust" has
a variety of connotations which often cannot be completely rendered by a
single English word.

[4] The epithet is understandable only as an antithesis to an unstated image
of intoxication and satiation on the part of those who know love's secrets.

praise the nourishment/Of body and blood" ("Hätten die Nüchternen/Einmal gekostet,/Alles verliessen sie,/Und setzten sich zu uns/An den Tisch der Sehnsucht,/Der nie leer wird./Sie erkennten der Liebe/Unendliche Fülle,/Und priesen die Nahrung/Von Leib und Blut").

In return for Christ's manifold gifts, the first song continues, the singer will remain "His humble child," an epithet important in understanding the poet's relationship to Christ. It is with the simple, trusting love of a child, filled with the assurance that his love is returned, that Novalis looks up to Christ. In a similarly naive fashion Novalis approaches the Virgin in the last two songs of the cycle, the introduction of Mary as the divine mother being anticipated earlier by frequent allusion to the Christ-child. Thus, when the poet begs in the fourteenth song for a vision of the Virgin, he appeals to her first as the mother of Christ and then as his own mother. The song reflects a desire to recapture fully the pure simplicity of childhood and to strip off any vestige of sophistication that would bar the singer from full communion with Christ and the Mother of Heaven. Fittingly, the final song of the cycle claims an intuitive, mystic knowledge of the divine that surpasses the scope of art and which can exist only in one who has recaptured the state of innocence for which the poet had longed.

With the same intuitive assurance Novalis goes on in the first song to claim the certain knowledge of the omnipresence of Christ, the conviction that He will be wherever two are gathered together —a Biblical phrase that returns in paraphrase in the ninth song when Novalis proclaims the resurrection of Christ. It is by extension of this image of omnipresent love, rather than as one persuaded by pantheistic doctrine, that Novalis depicts the presence of Christ in all things at other points in the cycle: "In cool streams . . . In fire's flames . . . In air and oil, in sounds and dew . . . From plants and stones and sea and light/Shimmers His childlike countenance./In all things His childlike activity" ("In kühlen Strömen . . . In Feuerflammen . . . In Luft und Öl, in Klang und Tau . . . Aus Kraut und Stein und Meer und Licht/Schimmert sein kindlich Angesicht./In allen Dingen sein kindlich Tun" [XII]), images which depict in their context a second Advent through the manifestation of Christ's love and life-giving power in nature.

Yet there are those who do not know Christ, and Novalis accordingly exhorts his fellow Christians to go out, disciple-like, and draw these into the Christian fold: "O, go out on every road/And bring in those who stray,/Stretch out to each one your hand/And happily invite them to us" ("O! geht hinaus auf allen Wegen,/Und holt die Irrenden herein,/Streckt jedem eure Hand entgegen,/Und ladet froh sie zu uns ein" [I]). The depiction of those who have not found the Saviour as "those who stray" revives the earlier images of uncertainty and darkness. The metaphor recurs later in the portrayal of the non-Christian: "He roams about alone, astray" ("Er schweift umher allein und irre" [III]), and again, more emphatically, when we are shown the frustrations of those who have failed to recognize the true goal of life (XI). The Christians, on the other hand, can proclaim "Heaven is with us on earth" ("Der Himmel ist bei uns auf Erden" [I]). It was Christ who, by His sacrifice, created on earth the "foundations of a Holy City" (XI) and made of the world an Eden again: "And blossoming eternally here/Springs forth the old Paradise" ("Und ewig blühend geht allhier/Das alte Paradies herfür" [XII]). In its sphere of reference this last image creates a bond between the images of a heaven on earth and those that express the life-giving power of Christ, the images of blossoming growth.

In the sixth stanza of the first song the poet turns from his individual experience to that of the Christian community, expanding his personal revelation into one of cosmic scope. This change is marked by an abrupt change of tense. As Novalis draws a metaphorical picture of the world before Christ's birth, we are reminded of the imagery of the fifth hymn to the night which depicts a fettered mankind ruled by an iron fate: "An old, heavy dream of sin/Was fettered to our hearts ... An iron bond held firmly to the earth/The quaking prisoners" ("Ein alter, schwerer Wahn von Sünde/War fest an unser Herz gebannt ... Ein eisern Band hielt an der Erde/Die bebenden Gefangnen fest" [I]). But the imagery, again, echoing the metaphor of the earlier stanzas, subtly relates this state to that of the poet before his discovery of Christ: "We strayed in the night like blind men,/Inflamed with repentance and desire simultaneously" ("Wir irrten in der Nacht wie Blinde,/Von Reu und Lust zugleich entbrannt" [I]). (This same equating of individual and universal experience is to be seen in the second, ninth, and eleventh song.) Every act seemed criminal, and man appeared to be "an enemy of the gods," while heaven revealed only death and suffering. Religious inspiration—"And if our spirits were illumined . . ." ("Und ward's in unserm Geiste helle . . ." [I]) (light imagery again represents the divine)—brought only dissatisfaction. All hope was consumed by the fear of death.

Once again Novalis returns to the theme of Christ's power to transform when in the eighth stanza he portrays the changes wrought in mankind by His coming. It was Christ who kindled in man a flame of new life, "ein allbelebend Feuer," that brought an awareness of his kinship with God. The revitalizing force of Christ is made particularly vivid in this image of resuscitating fire, a variant of which we find in the second song: "Finally there comes down to earth/The blessed child of heaven most high . . . Blows together into new, eternally bright flames/Sparks long scattered to the winds" ("Endlich kommt zur Erde nieder/Aller Himmel selges Kind . . . Weht zu neuen ewig lichten Flammen/Längst verstiebte Funken hier zusammen"). Implicit in these fire images is the consuming of the darkness that had made men blind to God and bound them to the earth, a metaphor then explicitly developed in the tenth song when Novalis praises the Cross as the symbol of Christ's love: "Go to that wondrous tree,/Give vent to quiet longing./From it proceeds a flame/That consumes the oppressive dream" ("Geh zu dem Wunderstamme,/Gib stiller Sehnsucht Raum,/Aus ihm geht eine Flamme/Und zehrt den schweren Traum"). It is with the light of the flame referred to in the eighth stanza that mankind has finally seen the real nature of heaven: "Only now did we see heaven open/As our old fatherland" ("Nun sahn wir erst den Himmel offen/Als unser altes Vaterland" [I]). Persuaded of man's divine origin, the poet foresees his return to this homeland of heaven.

The conviction that with Christ's coming mankind was freed from sin produces a joyful tone in the final stanzas of the first song. This faith was passed on from one generation to the next as a "birth-gift" ("Angebinde"), and thus life passed like a blissful dream in anticipation of eternal joy and love. Death, formerly a thing of terror, was scarcely noticed after Christ's sacrifice; the freeing of mankind from the death-horror is, for Novalis, the supreme "gift." It is of this that he sings in the triumphant ninth

song: "Down into the deep sea/Sank the horror of death/And each
of us may now see/Into his future, light and sublime" [5] ("Hinunter
in das tiefe Meer/Versank des Todes Graun,/Und jeder kann
nun leicht und hehr/In seine Zukunft schaun"). So sure of this
promise is Novalis that the horror of death is scarcely touched
upon in the cycle, and then only when it serves antithetically to
emphasize the joy of having Christ as Saviour. It is, instead, of
the bliss of life in Christ that Novalis sings, and his jubilation is
limited only by his recollection of the shame and suffering of the
Cross: "Moved by His crown of thorns/And by His faithfulness,
we weep" ("Gerührt von seinem Dornenkranze/Und seiner Treue
weinen wir" [I]). The poet's recognition that it was for him that
Christ suffered and died gives birth to a longing to endure the
same suffering (VIII), while in the sixth song he vows to stand
forever as a witness to this sacrifice.

The intensely personal relationship of Christian to Christ is
revealed throughout the cycle in a series of images which have
reference to the physical grasping of Christ by the individual, a
metaphorical relationship that has its roots in mystical experience.
Beginning with the image in the final stanza of the first song—
"We welcome every individual/Who with us grasps His hand"
("Ein jeder Mensch ist uns willkommen,/Der seine Hand mit uns
ergreift")—we meet a variety of expressions of this relationship.
Essentially the same image returns in the second song—"Reach
boldly for His hands" ("Greife dreist nach seinen Händen")—
while a somewhat different image in the third sheds further light
on the affinity of Christian to Christ: "And in any situation [you]
can confidently/Draw Him to your embrace" ("Und [du] kannst
getrost in jeder Lage/Ihn zärtlich in die Arme ziehn"). Related to
this group of images is the second song's "If you will only show
Him all your heart,/Like a faithful woman He will be yours"
("Wirst du nur das ganze Herz ihm zeigen,/Bleibt er wie ein treues
Weib dir eigen"). These metaphors of physical propinquity express

---

[5] The image of the death-horror sinking into the sea immediately suggests
an allusion to the setting of the sun. Here, perhaps, is an echo of the
hymns to the night. There the sun, the manifestation of light's power and
the symbol of time, is related to a belief that death is the end of existence.
This belief is destroyed with the metaphorical end of light. We find a
similar allusion in Klingsohr's "Märchen," cf. below, p. 124.

on the one hand a child-father relationship of man and Saviour—
echoed in the sixth song's "[We] weep bitterly and nestle/Childlike
at Thy knee" ("[Man] Weint bitterlich und schmieget/Sich kindlich an dein Knie")—and on the other hand a relationship of lover
and beloved, most poignantly represented in the erotic imagery of
the seventh song and evident in many references to Christ as "the
beloved."

Equally important in revealing Novalis' interpretation of the
relationship of man to Christ are the images of ripening growth
introduced by the final metaphor of the first song: "We welcome
every person/Who with us grasps His hand/And, taken up with
us in His heart,/Ripens into the fruit of Paradise" ("Ein jeder
Mensch ist uns willkommen,/Der seine Hand mit uns ergreift,/
Und in sein Herz mit aufgenommen/Zur Frucht des Paradieses
reift"). The complete dependency of the Christian upon Christ ist
conveyed through this image, yet at the same time there is the
implicit promise of attainment to perfection through Christ's love.
The fact of utter dependency is restated in similar, though more
conventional metaphor in the second song: "[You] must always
turn toward Him,/Blossom turning toward the sunshine" ("Musst
dich immer nach ihm wenden,/Blüte nach dem Sonnenschein").
The same song expands the image to characterize earth as the
garden of God wherein mankind grows and develops: "And so
let us in God's full garden/Await faithfully every bud and flower"
("Und so lasst im vollen Gottesgarten/Treu uns jede Knosp' und
Blüte warten"). From the same area of reference Novalis draws
an equally conventional image depicting his condition before the
hour in which Christ was revealed to him: "As if stung by a worm/
My heart and blossom wilted" ("Wie von einem Wurm gestochen,
/Welke Herz und Blüte mir" [IV]), and in the ninth song, as he
heralds the resurrected Christ, he employs yet another image of
flowering growth to express the hope given the individual: "To
every good deed everyone/May glow anew,/For magnificently
will this seed/Bloom in more lovely lea" ("Es kann zu jeder guten
Tat/Ein jeder frischer glühn,/Denn herrlich wird ihm diese Saat/
In schönern Fluren blühn"). Finally these images of eventual
fruition are joined with those growth images that depict Christ's
life-giving power when this last metaphor is developed to correlate
the rebirth of the world through Christ and the reawakening of

the world in Spring: "He lives and will now be with us/When all else forsakes us!/And thus this day for us shall be/A festival of universal rejuvenation" ("Er lebt, und wird nun bei uns sein,/ Wenn alles uns verlässt!/Und so soll dieser Tag uns sein/Ein Weltverjüngungsfest").

Thus, from the images introduced in the first song, Novalis develops a pattern of imagery that gives unity to the group, a prime function of his imagery here as in his other works. In this instance, as is evident from this analysis, Novalis exploits traditional images, many of these being even more conventional than the ones to which we have made reference—the heart as the seat of man's emotions, the tears that represent the individual's grief, and many others. The mode of expression he chooses for these songs is simple and direct, his themes familiar, his verse forms exoteric. His metaphor thus has the virtue of being suited to its context. The familiar imagery, too, seems to serve the poet's felt need for expressing his relationship to his fellow Christians. It is through the imagery, essentially, that he shows the universal quality of his own experience. The metaphors and epithets so frequently invoked in the Christian hymn have been hallowed by constant use and have become, so to speak, a part of the Church's ritual. These Novalis seems to have adopted even as at this point he wholeheartedly embraced the tenets of the Christian tradition.

There are, however, in the songs certain images which seem to be part of a fixed system of private symbols. Certain metaphors to which attention has been drawn in this analysis—the image of a blossoming polar region; the sun as a symbol of secularism; the representation of a life without Christ as an oppressive dream; the image of a life-giving flame that rises from the grave—all recur in other Hardenbergian contexts. We may surmise that the ideas thus represented had become fixedly embodied in the respective images and that these metaphors suggested themselves at once to the poet. As often, when carried away by his emotional belief in the inspirational quality of sexual love, Novalis invokes, as in the seventh song particularly, the drastic erotic imagery that characterizes much of his other poetry. While such images, as well as his metaphors of tactile cognition, have their counterparts in the songs of the Christian mystics, the extensive use of this imagery by Novalis, here and elsewhere, points to its having private symbolic value for him. Thus, even within the relatively simple framework of his sacred songs, it is to his private symbols that Novalis turns, subconsciously perhaps, to reveal the most profound and poignantly felt moments of his religious experience.

CHAPTER VI

"DIE ERWARTUNG"—*HEINRICH VON OFTERDINGEN (I)*

The Romantic interpretation of the spirit of the Middle Ages is nowhere better exemplified than in a passage in the second chapter of Novalis' *Heinrich von Ofterdingen:* "At all moments of change, as though in an interregnum, a higher, spiritual power seems to be about to burst forth; and just as on the surface of our world those areas richest in treasures both above and below ground are to be found situated in the middle between the wild, inhospitable, age-old mountains and the boundless plains, so the period between the crude ages of barbarism and the age of art, knowledge and wealth is occupied by a time profound and romantic, a time which conceals beneath its simple garb a nobler mien. Who does not love to wander in the twilight, when night and light shatter against one another, creating richer shades and colors? And so we gladly plunge into the age when Heinrich lived . . ." (I, 110). For Novalis, the "middle" period, coming between the time of barbarism and the modern age, was a time when the truly romantic spirit made itself manifest, when the hidden splendor of the physical world was revealed, and the physical and spiritual realms flowed together as do day and night in twilight. The poet's ardent enthusiasm for the spirit of the Middle Ages, so evident in this passage, seems to have developed through his study, in the spring of 1799, of chronicles on the age of the Emperor Friedrich II. It would seem likely that he read at that point Johannes Rothe's *Thüringsche Chronik* and *Leben der heiligen Elizabeth,* in both of which appears the figure of the semi-legendary poet Heinrich von Ofterdingen. (The variant spelling, "Afterdingen," used on occasion by Novalis, is to be found in Rothe). References in the author's notes indicate that he proposed to use in his novel certain elements of the Ofterdingen legend, particularly the familiar story of the contest of poets at the Wartburg. However, Novalis' work breaks off when Ofterdingen's career as a poet has scarcely begun. There is thus little connection between the Ofterdingen of legend and the youthful hero of Novalis. Except for the figures of the poet Klingsohr and of Ofterdingen's patroness, Sophie, Countess of Thuringia, Novalis' fragment owes nothing to legend. His Heinrich von Ofterdingen is his own creation.

It seems probable that Novalis began work on *Heinrich von Ofterdingen* in the late part of 1799 after the *Hymnen an die Nacht* and the *Geistliche Lieder* were completed. By February 1800 he was able to inform Ludwig Tieck of substantial progress: "My novel is in full swing . . . I have the whole plan pretty nearly worked out in my head. There will be two books—the first will be finished in three weeks, I hope. It contains intimations and the basis of the action of the second part. The whole is to be an apotheosis of poetry. Heinrich von Ofterdingen reaches maturity as a poet in the first part, and in the second part he is transfigured as a poet" (IV, 330). Some three weeks later, as Novalis had anticipated, the first part of the novel, "Expectation" ("Die Erwartung"), was completed; but the poet's work on the second part, "Fulfillment" ("Die Erfüllung"), was retarded and then halted by his contraction of tuberculosis, the disease that was to take his life. The fragmentary novel was published for the first time in the first volume of Novalis' works in 1802, together with Tieck's account of the author's plan for the completion of the work. Care must be exercised in evaluating Tieck's sketch. He seems to have done little more than link together in arbitrary fashion details of notes made by Novalis. Even these notes are not to be considered completely reliable. According to Friedrich Schlegel, Novalis changed his mind constantly about his plans. This uncertainty is apparent in the notes themselves. Clearly, we cannot know which of the many notes and sketches made by Novalis were ever given serious consideration after their initial conception. Any postulation of the author's plans for the second part must therefore be based first and foremost on evidence in "Die Erwartung." This, as Novalis indicated to Tieck in the letter cited above, contains "intimations and the basis of the action of the second part." However, attention will be drawn in this and the following chapters to the several instances of correspondence between the author's notes and elements of the text.

As Novalis wrote to Tieck, the first part of his apotheosis of poetry depicts the preparation of Heinrich von Ofterdingen for his rôle as a poet, while the second part was to have shown his transfiguration. Thus in "Die Erwartung" we see the gradual unfolding of the hero under the many influences to which he is exposed and the emergence of the poetic spirit within and about him. The youthful Heinrich of this first part is essentially a passive character. The substance of the work at this point lies in his reaction to the forces and influences that shape him. The words of Klingsohr to Heinrich in Chapter VII make explicit the fact that the action of the first part is symbolic: "I have marked well that the spirit of poetry is your friendly companion ... In the vicinity of the poet poetry everywhere bursts forth. The land of poetry, the romantic Orient, has greeted you with its sweet melancholy; you have been addressed by war in its wild splendor, and nature and history have crossed your path in the shape of a miner and a recluse" (I, 187). Thus we see that each of the characters with whom Heinrich comes in contact typifies in some way an important aspect of man's emotional or intellectual life. Except for some few realistic passages which serve to further the action or create a background to the action the work is purely symbolic. The inclusion of dreams and fables, which might at first seem to have little immediate reference to the larger context, contributes to this character. An important premise of the work, revealed in the first part by allusion, is the belief that all things are one, that the spirit of the whole is revealed in the individual part, and that all things exist in one another. To this idea is joined the concept of metempsychosis; thus it is that Ofterdingen feels that he has known before the individuals with whom he comes face to face and that he is reliving experiences which belong to a past existence. It would thus seem probable that in "Die Erfüllung" Novalis intended to show how the sympathy existing between all things, past, present and future, immanent and transcendent, may be revealed through poetry.

In this symbolic action implicit statement, through imagery, is of paramount importance. One must assume that the several images that run through the first part, becoming symbols as they link action at various levels, were to be developed and resolved in the completed work. The images of the dreams and fables, I shall show, have particular significance. In some instances these portend

the events of Heinrich's life, while in other cases explicit themes of
the conversations in which the hero participates are presented in
the metaphor of the fables. It is essentially through parallelism
of the imagery that the dreams and fables are linked to the larger
context, while the imagery of Klingsohr's "Märchen" serves as a
bridge between "Die Erwartung" and "Die Erfüllung." Moreover,
the flowering of the poetic spirit in Heinrich is revealed through
his increasing propensity to think in poetic images. It is to an
examination of the implicit content of this imagery and of its
function in its context, rather than to the author's more explicit
statements, that this study of *Heinrich von Ofterdingen* is primarily
directed. This analysis, I believe, will show that Novalis' purpose
and attitudes are most clearly revealed through his imagery and
that the images of the first part in many instances suggests the
course of action of the completed work.

The action of "Die Erwartung" depicts Heinrich's journey from
his home in Thuringia, his meeting successively with merchants,
Crusaders, a Saracen maiden, a miner, a recluse, and finally with
the poet Klingsohr and the latter's daughter Mathilde at his grandfather's home in Augsburg. While Novalis here follows a tradition
of the eighteenth-century novel, this journey is itself symbolic—a
journey from the limited horizons, the sober and rationalistic world
of the hero's home (a world where poetry cannot flourish), to the
land of Klingsohr, the land of poetry and intoxication. In the
reactions of Heinrich's parents to his dream of the blue flower,
depicted in the first chapter, we see that the atmosphere of his
home is hostile to the emergence of the poetic spirit. Heinrich is
sufficiently imaginative and responsive to express the belief that
he had experienced no "mere dream." Yet his statement evokes
from his mother only the response that a physiological explanation
exists for the phenomenon of dreams. The reply of his father
reveals a narrowly rationalistic approach to such questions:
"Dreams are idle fancies, no matter what your so-called learned
gentlemen think of them, and you would be well advised to turn
your mind away from such useless and harmful reflections"
("Träume sind Schäume, mögen auch die hochgelahrten Herren
davon denken, was sie wollen, und du tust wohl, wenn du dein
Gemüt von dergleichen unnützen und schädlichen Betrachtungen
abwendest" [I, 104]). He goes on to deny the existence of prophetic

vision and mystical knowledge, claiming that knowledge of the divine can come only through reason and ethics. The fact that he has all but forgotten the details of a youthful dream, that had predicted he could enjoy "the highest earthly lot" as an artist, shows how his own imaginative powers have been extinguished by the ordered and routine existence he has created for himself as a craftsman. He is representative of the artist destroyed by his concern for the material aspects of existence and by suppression of his imaginative powers in placing craftsmanship above inspiration. Clearly, Heinrich's father, who wishes his son to follow in his footsteps, represents a danger to the youth's poetic gifts. It is perhaps the unconscious sensing of this danger that prompts his mother, a daughter of the land of poetry to the south, to remove Heinrich from this atmosphere.

The images of Heinrich's dream point forward to the action of the second part of the novel and I shall therefore discuss them fully later. Suffice it to say that the similarity of the images in the dreams of father and son indicates that these have symbolic value and that the blue flower seen by both has particular meaning for Heinrich's existence. Though his future is to be dominated by the search for its meaning, Heinrich is as yet naive, his intuitive powers dormant. His premonitions regarding the significance of the flower crystallize only when he comes directly in contact with the spirit of love and poetry in the person of Mathilde. The final image of the father's dream, however, has immediate reference to Heinrich's future, portending as it does some wondrous fate for the youth: ". . . I saw before me your mother with an amiable and bashful look; she bore a radiant child in her arms and she held it out to me, when suddenly the child grew visibly, became ever more luminous and more radiant, and finally soared above us on dazzling white wings, took both of us in its arms and flew so high with us that the earth looked merely like a golden bowl with the neatest carving on it" (". . . ich sah deine Mutter mit freundlichem, verschämtem Blick vor mir; sie hielt ein glänzendes Kind in den Armen, und reichte mir es hin, als auf einmal das Kind zusehends wuchs, immer heller und glänzender ward, und sich endlich mit blendendweissen Flügeln über uns erhob, uns beide in seinen Arm nahm, und so hoch mit uns flog, dass die Erde nur wie eine goldene Schüssel mit dem saubersten Schnitzwerk aussah" [I, 108]).

Heinrich's dream, following upon the visit of a stranger who told him of the blue flower and upon his recollection of other stories of a time when men conversed with plants and animals— an image of a Golden Age that is a familiar one in Novalis—has served to bring him into touch for the first time with the realm of fantasy and to prepare him for the maturing process that will make him a poet. On the eve of his journey (Chapter II) Heinrich is twenty, on the threshold of manhood, a naive and inexperienced youth whose life thus far has been confined to the environs of his home. His knowledge of the world comes largely from his instruction under the chaplain of the Thuringian court and he clings to his familiar surroundings while at the same time looking forward to the adventure that lies before him: "He beheld himself standing on the threshold of the far-off land into which he had often gazed in vain from the nearby mountains and which he had pictured to himself in strange colors. He was on the point of plunging into its blue waters. The magic flower stood before him, and he looked across to Thuringia, which he was now leaving behind him, with the strange presentiment that after long wanderings he would return to his homeland from that region to which their journey was now taking them, as though his goal were in fact his home" ("Er sah sich an der Schwelle der Ferne, in die er oft vergebens von den nahen Bergen geschaut, und die er sich mit sonderbaren Farben ausgemalt hatte. Er war im Begriff, sich in ihre blaue Flut zu tauchen. Die Wunderblume stand vor ihm, und er sah nach Thüringen, welches er jetzt hinter sich liess, mit der seltsamen Ahndung hinüber, als werde er nach langen Wanderungen von der Weltgegend her, nach welcher sie jetzt reisten, in sein Vaterland zurückkommen, und als reise er daher diesem eigentlich zu" [I, 111]). Implicit in these words is the image of a path that leads back to its starting point. If we reflect that the individual, changed and enriched by his experience as he follows this path, must return to his point of origin at a different level, we see that this is a spiral image. This image, which we meet at later points in the fragment, would seem to be the basic structural image of the novel.

Heinrich's journey is undertaken with his mother in the company of a group of merchants, the first of the voices of poetry that are to appear about the young man. The merchants, I suggest, personify the inquiring, mercantile spirit that throughout history has led man to leave his familiar surroundings to explore new realms. In conversation with them Heinrich reveals his intuitive nature as he states his belief in two paths to knowledge. The first is an empirical method, "der Weg der Erfahrung," the second by means of introspection and direct observation of nature. His claim that the latter affords immediate knowledge of the nature of things and an ability to divine the sympathy of all things for one another prompts the merchants to exclaim that Heinrich has poetic gifts (a statement so often repeated in the work that it becomes redundant). As a discussion of the nature of poetry ensues and the merchants narrate fables to illustrate their viewpoints, Heinrich is brought into direct contact with poetry for the first time. The merchants recount how they had heard fables in which was revealed how poets had harmonized opposing forces and had given form to the world of nature that had previously been wild and hostile: "Only since that time, so legend has it, are the varied musical sounds and the strange sympathies and order patterns supposed to have come into nature, everything before then having been wild, disordered and hostile" ("Seitdem sollen, wie die Sage lautet, erst die mannigfaltigen Töne und die sonderbaren Sympathien und Ordnungen in die Natur gekommen sein, indem vorher alles wild, unordentlich und feindselig gewesen ist" [I, 117]). In illustration of this argument the merchants tell first the story of the Greek poet Arion. (The name Arion is not mentioned in the story, however, presumably in order that the poet may better serve as a symbol of poetry itself.) In this familiar story is made manifest the power of the poet to sway men and animals, and poetry overcomes hostile, destructive forces represented by the avaricious sailors and the sea monsters. Implicit in both the fable and in the prior remarks of the merchants is an image of two hostile forces at work in the universe—the one a wild, chaotic, destructive element antagonistic to poetry; the other, the spirit of poetry itself, an ordering and harmonizing force. Thus we meet at its introduction an image that is developed throughout the fragment and which would again seem to point forward to the action of the second part.

Explicit and implicit statement walk hand in hand in the early chapters of *Heinrich von Ofterdingen*. The imagery of the Arion fable complements the claims made by the merchants, presenting these in palpable form. Gradually implicit statement, through imagery, assumes the dominant rôle in the fragment, culminating in the symbolism of Klingsohr's "Märchen." This tendency is furthered in the telling of the fable of Atlantis (Chapter III), the imagery of which expands the theme of poetry's power to unite apparently dissimilar realms. But it also presages the action of the novel and, indeed, points to the symbolic meaning of this action. Taken literally, the story of Atlantis is a simple one. It is only through the interpretation of its imagery with reference to the larger context that its symbolic value in the work becomes clear.

The merchants first describe a court of great magnificence ruled by a king with two great passions: "The old king ... had two concerns which were the real reasons for the existence of this magnificent court and to which the court owed its beautiful style of life. One was his affection for his daughter, who was infinitely dear to him both because she reminded him of his wife (who had died while still young) and because she herself was an indescribably lovable girl. He would gladly have sacrificed all of nature's treasures and all the powers of the human spirit in order to provide a heaven on earth for her. The other was a genuine passion for poetry and the masters of that art" ("Der alte König ... hatte zwei Neigungen, die der wahre Anlass dieser prächtigen Hofhaltung waren, und denen sie ihre schöne Einrichtung zu danken hatte. Eine war die Zärtlichkeit für seine Tochter, die ihm als Andenken seiner früh verstorbenen Gemahlin und als ein unaussprechlich liebenswürdiges Mädchen unendlich teuer war, und für die er gern alle Schätze der Natur und alle Macht des menschlichen Geistes aufgeboten hätte, um ihr einen Himmel auf Erden zu verschaffen. Die andere war eine wahre Leidenschaft für die Dichtkunst und ihre Meister" [I, 119]). The juxtaposition of these two passions inevitably forces the reader to equate them in his mind. That the princess does in fact symbolize the spirit of poetry is subsequently revealed in the fable by the metaphor: "His daughter had grown up surrounded by song and her very soul had become a delicate melody ... thus she was regarded as the visible spirit of that magnificent art" ("Seine Tochter war unter Gesängen aufgewachsen, und ihre ganze Seele war ein zartes Lied geworden ...

so hielt man sie für die sichtbare Seele jener herrlichen Kunst"
[I, 119 f]). In this land where poetry holds sway the benevolent
powers of song have vanquished all hostile and destructive elements: "They enjoyed life in slow sips as though it were a precious
wine and with so much the more feeling of comfort since all
objectionable and odious passions had been dispelled like discords
by the gentle, harmonious mood that prevailed in all hearts. Peace
of mind . . . had become the possession of this wonderful age, and
discord appeared only in the poet's old lays as a former enemy of
man" ("Man genoss das Leben mit langsamen, kleinen Zügen wie
einen köstlichen Trank, und mit desto reinerem Wohlbehagen, da
alle widrige gehässige Leidenschaften wie Misstöne von der sanften
harmonischen Stimmung verscheucht wurden, die in allen Ge-
mütern herrschend war. Frieden der Seele . . . war das Eigentum
dieser wunderbaren Zeit geworden, und die Zwietracht erschien nur
in den alten Sagen der Dichter, als eine ehmalige Feindin der Menschen" [I, 120]). Yet one element of disquiet threatens the happiness
of this otherwise blissful land. All are concerned that the princess
be happily married so that this idyllic state may be perpetuated.
But the vanity of the king prevents any suitor from seeking his
daughter's hand. The king, we learn, had come from the East, his
wife was a descendant of the Persian hero, Rustam, and the poets
had told him of his relationship to the earlier supernatural rulers
of the world: ". . . in the magic mirror of their art the disparity
between his origins and those of other men and the magnificence
of his family had been made even more plain" (". . . in dem Zau-
berspiegel ihrer Kunst war ihm der Abstand seiner Herkunft von
dem Ursprunge der andern Menschen, die Herrlichkeit seines
Stammes noch heller erschienen" [I, 121]). Thus, the imagery
suggests, the advent of an eternal Golden Age is being prevented
because the spirit of poetry is held apart from the force to which
it should be wedded. Unless the princess is married she will wilt
and waste away, despite the magnificence of her surroundings.
This, then, is the problem of the fable embodied in allegory—to
what can the spirit of poetry be wedded in order that the longed
for Golden Age may appear?

In the woods near the palace dwell two men, father and son,
whose simple home amidst natural surroundings contrasts vividly
with the splendor of the court. The two devote themselves to the

study and observation of nature, using the knowledge gained to help others. Their pursuits have kept them from contact with the palace. Indeed, the realms of palace and hut are not linked together until the princess happens upon the home of these students of nature while walking in the woods. The first glimpse of a world unknown to her has a profound effect upon the princess: "A magic veil draped in broad folds about her undimmed consciousness. It seemed to her as though, when the veil were lifted, she would find herself in a supernatural world" ("Ein magischer Schleier dehnte sich in weiten Falten um ihr klares Bewusstsein. Es war ihr, als würde sie sich, wenn er aufgeschlagen würde, in einer überirdischen Welt befinden" [I, 123]). Equally profound is the impact upon her of the court at her return. She is almost shocked by its splendor and its colorful life. The gulf between the two realms would appear unspannable. After the departure of the princess, who has concealed her identity, the youth finds a jewel she had worn, which we learn later was "a talisman which assured the safety of her person, for she could never unwillingly come under the domination of another so long as she had it in her possession" ("ein Talisman . . ., dessen Besitz ihr die Freiheit ihrer Person sicherte, indem sie damit nie in fremde Gewalt ohne ihren Willen geraten konnte" [I, 125]). In gazing at the jewel the youth is stirred for the first time to express his emotions in words. His poem (I, 124) reveals that he has recognized in the jewel the symbol of the princess' heart. Love has unsealed his lips and at the same time has endowed him with what many allusions in the novel suggest is a prime attribute of the true poet—the faculty of divining the relationship between things and of expressing this relationship in poetic images.

The princess pays many more visits to the hut, still not revealing her identity, and love draws youth and princess closer together. While he reveals to her the secrets of nature, she instructs him in the art of poetry. After their love has been consummated the princess, her identity now revealed, stays at the hut to await the birth of her child. Her absence from the court transforms its life, robbing her people of their peace and happiness, and rendering the king disconsolate: "Only when his minstrels came before him in the evenings and offered their beautiful songs did it seem the old joy could be recaptured. His daughter seemed close at

hand . . ." ("Nur wenn abends seine Sänger vor ihn kamen und
schöne Lieder mitbrachten, war es, als liesse sich die alte Freude
wieder vor ihm blicken; seine Tochter dünkte ihm nah . . ." [I,
128]). Yet, although the songs seem to bring his daughter closer
to him, with the spirit of poetry departed the songs of the court
are without content: "Nothing can take my daughter's place. Without her even the songs are nothing but empty words and illusion.
She was the magic that gave them life and joy, power and form"
("Meine Tochter kann mir nichts ersetzen. Ohne sie sind auch die
Gesänge nichts, als leere Worte und Blendwerk. Sie war der
Zauber, der ihnen Leben und Freude, Macht und Gestalt gab"
[I, 128]). As the spring approaches, however, the people whisper
that the princess will return. (The advent of the Golden Age is
symbolized at other points in the fragment by the dawn of an
eternal spring.) One year after her departure a feast is held in
anticipation of this event. After the court poets have ended their
songs a strange voice breaks the expectant silence, the voice of the
youth who has entered the company: "The voice was extra-
ordinarily beautiful and the song displayed a strange and wonderful character. It dealt with the origins of the world, of the stars,
plants, animals and man, with the almighty sympathy of nature,
with the ancient Golden Age and its rulers, Love and Poetry, with
the appearance of hatred and barbarism and their struggles against
those benevolent goddesses, and finally the song told of the future
triumph of the latter, of the end of misery, the rejuvenation of
nature and the return of an eternal Golden Age" ("Die Stimme war
ausserordentlich schön, und der Gesang trug ein fremdes, wunder-
bares Gepräge. Er handelte von dem Ursprunge der Welt, von der
Entstehung der Gestirne, der Pflanzen, Tiere und Menschen, von
der allmächtigen Sympathie der Natur, von der uralten, goldenen
Zeit und ihren Beherrscherinnen, der Liebe und Poesie, von der
Erscheinung des Hasses und der Barbarei und ihren Kämpfen mit
jenen wohltätigen Göttinnen, und endlich von dem zukünftigen
Triumph der letztern, dem Ende der Trübsale, der Verjüngung der
Natur und der Wiederkehr eines ewigen goldenen Zeitalters" [I,
130]). Such a song had never before been heard. It is a new, all-
embracing poetry that represents the union of the spirit of ancient
poetry that had its origins in the East with the spirit of nature and
the natural sciences, symbolized in the union of the princess and

the youth. (For Novalis, I suggest, this represents the spirit of true Romantic poetry.)

As the youth sings again—a song paraphrasing the story of himself and the princess and designed to move the king to forgiveness—the youth's father appears with the princess, her child on her arm. His song ended, he raises the veil that hides the princess' face to reunite the king with his daughter. Let us refer again to the words that describe the emotions of the princess at her first encounter with the youth: "A magic veil draped in broad folds about her undimmed consciousness. It seemed to her as though, when the veil were lifted, she would find herself in a supernatural world" [I, 123]. This "magic" veil, like the one that concealed her face, has now been raised. A new world is ushered in, a Golden Age that is to be perpetuated into eternity. The spirit of this new age is personified in the child of the youth and princess, and as the king takes the child in his arms old and new worlds are joined. In the child the king senses the divine inspiration of the spirit that will rule the everlasting Golden Age: "The king took the child and with touching devotion held it up toward heaven . . . The poets broke into song and the evening became a sacred eve for the entire land, where life henceforth was one beautiful celebration" ("Der König nahm das Kind und reichte es mit rührender Andacht gen Himmel . . . In Gesänge brachen die Dichter aus, und der Abend ward ein heiliger Vorabend dem ganzen Lande, dessen Leben fortan nur e in schönes Fest war" [I, 134]).

The voice of poetry itself has now spoken directly to Heinrich in these fables, yet its words are not at this point fully understood by him. His latent poetic gifts must be developed through further experiences and growth, represented in the action of the novel by his meeting successively with the spirit of the Crusades, the spirit of the East, of the natural sciences, and of history. At the next stage in his journey (Chapter IV) Heinrich is introduced into the household of an old warrior, who, with the companions he keeps about him in a life of revelry, had participated in a Crusade. In this household Heinrich comes face to face with two polarities, symbolized by two objects placed in his hands—a sword and a lute. On the one hand is the warrior with his retinue, their virile, aggressive confidence representing a Christendom militant and triumphant. The nature of the Crusaders is best revealed in such metaphor of their song of the Cross as "Soon we shall wash in joyous mood/The holy grave with heathen blood" ("Wir waschen bald in frohem Mute/Das heilige Grab mit Heidenblute" [I, 138]) and in an image, in the penultimate stanza of the song, that depicts the Virgin hovering, Valkyrie-like, over the field of battle. The sight and touch of the sword placed in his hand by the Crusaders and the vicarious experience of war excite Heinrich. He is made aware of irrational forces in man he had not known before. Similarly, there is a release of new powers within himself. That this experience contributes to the growth of the poetic spirit within him is suggested by the fact that his thoughts seem to crystallize naturally in poetic images: "the grave appeared to him as a pale, noble, youthful figure sitting on a great stone amid a wild mob and being abused in a horrible manner; it seemed as though this figure looked with grievous face toward a cross that shimmered in light outline in the background and that in the moving waves of an ocean took on an infinite variety of shapes" ("das Grab kam ihm wie eine bleiche, edle, jugendliche Gestalt vor, die auf einem grossen Stein mitten unter wildem Pöbel sässe, und auf eine entsetzliche Weise gemisshandelt würde, als wenn sie mit kummervollem Gesichte nach einem Kreuze blicke, was im Hintergrunde mit lichten Zügen schimmerte, und sich in den bewegten Wellen eines Meeres unendlich vervielfältigte" [I, 138]).

The rough, masculine world of the Crusaders has its antithesis in the gentle, exotic spirit of the East, personified in Zulima, a young Saracen maiden brought back from the Holy Land as a prisoner. Her song (I, 139f) of longing for her homeland, of the brutality of the Crusaders, and of her personal grief moves Heinrich to compassion. As Zulima sees in him the likeness of her brother, a young poet, the sympathy between the two is immediate and profound. It was the premise of the Atlantis fable that poetry had its origins in the East. Now, as Zulima speaks of the wonders of the Orient and eventually places a lute in Heinrich's hands, a link between this girl and the fable is readily established in the mind of the reader.

The stringed instrument—in this case a lute—serves Novalis as a symbol both of the poet's calling and of the powers of poetry. The princess of the Atlantis fable and Fabel in Klingsohr's "Märchen" accompany their songs on lute or lyre. Heinrich's confused emotional state just before his encounter with the Saracen maid is accompanied by a vague longing for a lute. Remarkably, at this point he does not know what a lute is or what effect it produces. He declines the Saracen girl's offer of her lute, this refusal indicating an unconscious realization on Heinrich's part that his poetic powers are not as yet unleashed. Later Klingsohr tells Heinrich that Mathilde will instruct him in playing the guitar, while in the second part of the novel Heinrich, now a poet, appears with lute in hand.

Heinrich's meeting with Zulima would again seem to portend events in Heinrich's future and be of ultimately greater significance for the action of the novel than merely to make Heinrich aware of the wonders of the East. She tells him of the beauty, the harmony of a long-populated land: "There is a special charm to living on ground long populated and previously given lustre by diligence, activity and affection. Nature seems there to have become more human and more understandable" ("Das Leben auf einem längst bewohnten und ehemals schon durch Fleiss, Tätigkeit und Neigung verherrlichten Boden hat einen besondern Reiz. Die Natur scheint dort menschlicher und verständlicher geworden" [I, 142]). Her words suggest that the chaotic force in nature to which we have earlier referred has been subdued in her native land, as it had been in the land of Atlantis. The harmonizing rôle that was perhaps to have been played by Heinrich's poetry in the completed novel may be foreshadowed in Zulima's hope for a reconciliation of the hostile worlds of Christian and Moslem: "Our princes ardently respected the grave of your Holy One, whom we too regard as a divine prophet; and how wonderfully His holy grave could have been the cradle of a happy understanding, the occasion of everlasting beneficent alliances!" ("Unsere Fürsten ehrten andachtsvoll das Grab eures Heiligen, den auch wir für einen göttlichen Propheten halten; und wie schön hätte sein heiliges Grab die Wiege eines glücklichen Einverständnisses, der Anlass ewiger wohltätiger Bündnisse werden können!" [I, 142f]).

The miner and the recluse who next cross Heinrich's path (Chapter V) characterize what for Novalis are related aspects of man's intellectual activity. Both the natural sciences and history, in Novalis' eyes, serve to give man deeper understanding of his relationship to nature. The subterranean depths in which these two individuals spend their lives have symbolic value for the poet. The miner's realm—the dark, relatively unknown depths of the earth—suggests a world of mysteries and hidden wealth that can be revealed only to those bold enough to venture its exploration. The miner's intimate contact with nature through his study of the earth's strata has given him empirical knowledge of the laws and forces at work in nature. At the same time his naive inquisitiveness and humility have preserved within him childlike intuitive powers that reveal to him the relationship of man and nature, a relationship depicted in his song allegorizing the nature of gold: "Ich kenne wo ein festes Schloss . . ." (I, 153f). Heinrich's appreciation of the vastness and infinite variety of nature is intensified as he listens to the miner's account of his life and work. Once again the experience has the effect of evoking poetic images within him: "The old man's words had opened within him a tapestry-concealed door. He saw his little parlor built close by a lofty cathedral, while from the cathedral's stone floor rose up the stern world of the past to be greeted by the clear, happy future in the form of golden angel images, singing and hovering in the dome . . . How astonished he was that this clear sight, so indispensible for his existence, had so long escaped him! Suddenly now he saw in proper perspective all his relationships to the great world about him . . ." ("Die Worte des Alten hatten eine versteckte Tapetentür in ihm geöffnet. Er sah sein kleines Wohnzimmer dicht an einen erhabenen Münster gebaut, aus dessen steinernem Boden die ernste Vorwelt emporstieg, während von der Kuppel die klare fröhliche Zukunft in goldnen Engelskindern ihr singend entgegenschwebte . . . Wie wunderte er sich, dass ihm diese klare, seinem Dasein schon unentbehrliche Ansicht so lange fremd geblieben war! Nun übersah er auf einmal alle seine Verhältnisse mit der weiten Welt um ihn her . . ." [I, 156f]). The image of a tapestry-concealed door brings to life the picture of a carefully hidden entrance to a secret passage way. Succinctly, yet dramatically, Novalis conveys to us the impression that the miner's words have penetrated depths of Heinrich's soul that the latter had not known the existence of. For the first time the young man grasps the relationship of his own limited and familiar world (the parlor) to the splendid new world being opened to him (the cathedral). The relationship, too, of past, present, and future bursts upon him. He recalls the Atlantis fable and a thousand other things that are now brought into meaningful harmony.

The image in the passage quoted above of past and future joining together is recalled in the words of the recluse, who describes history as "the secret concatenation of past and future" ("die geheime Verkettung des Ehemaligen und Künftigen" [I, 162]). The recluse, Friedrich von Hohenzollern, a former Crusader, has devoted his life to study and meditation since the death of his wife and two children. From him Heinrich learns of the wealth of past ages and also of the relationship of poetry to history, when the recluse insists that historians must be poets if they are to do justice to their task: ". . . for only poets can thoroughly understand that art of linking events together properly" (I, 163f). The subterranean cave where Hohenzollern makes his home characterizes not only his voluntary isolation from the rest of mankind but also his penetration to the depths of hidden knowledge. This chosen habitat, too, immediately establishes a bond between the recluse and the miner. The relationship of the latter's pursuits to the study of history is emphasized in the conversation between Hohenzollern and the miner, in which once more the implicit image of two hostile forces in nature is called to mind as they speak of the gradual taming and ordering of nature in past ages. The most significant incident of this episode, however, is Heinrich's discovery in Hohenzollern's library of a book written in the Provençal dialect. Of this book, that had been brought back from the Holy Land, Hohenzollern says: "As far as I know, it is a novel about the wonderful fate of a poet in which poetry is praised and depicted in its various aspects. The end of this manuscript is missing" (I, 170). Though Heinrich cannot read the text he turns the pages to find his own person in the illustrations. There he sees himself in the company of many people, some known and some as yet unknown by name, though again strangely familiar. Certain pictures recall the visions of his dream. In many he sees himself in the company of a noble man and a beautiful girl. Although the end of the book is missing Heinrich seems to know what his fate will be—a feeling that he is reliving a life lived before.

The book seems to have particular significance in the novel. As Heinrich sees himself in the illustrations of this "novel of the wonderful fate of a poet" it would seem that he is seeing the face of all poets. Heinrich, like all the other characters in the work, is himself a symbolic figure. Novalis' hero is the poet of all generations. In portraying his fate Novalis is seeking to depict what is universal in the fate of all poets. When we recall that Novalis described *Heinrich von Ofterdingen* itself as an "apotheosis of poetry" Hohenzollern's description of this book—"a novel ... in which poetry is praised and depicted in its various aspects"—assumes further significance. Novalis would seem to suggest that his own novel is a restatement of the one true theme of poetry, the praise of the spirit of poetry in all its manifestations. In view of the fact that Novalis' novel remained a fragment at his death Hohenzollern's closing words—"The end of this manuscript is missing"— have a poignantly ironic quality.

Hohenzollern seems to know of his own implication in Heinrich's destiny, for he speaks of a future meeting. (Allusion to this future meeting is also made in Novalis' notes: "Count von Hohenzollern and the merchants return too" ("Der Graf von Hohenzollern und die Kaufleute kommen auch wieder" [I, 241]). It is suggested in the words of Hohenzollern's daughter in the second part that Heinrich is also Hohenzollern's dead son restored to life.) As the travelers depart Hohenzollern says: "If you fix your eyes firmly on heaven you will never lose your way home" ("Wenn euer Auge fest am Himmel haftet, so werdet ihr nie den Weg zu eurer Heimat verlieren" [I, 170]). Once again we meet the implicit spiral image, expanded in this case to suggest the universality of experience of all individuals.

Heinrich's journey and his experiences have brought him now to the threshold of his life as a poet. The sixth chapter begins with the delineation of the contrast between active, aggressive individuals, "people born to action and industry" ("Menschen, die zum Handeln, zur Geschäftigkeit geboren sind" [I, 170]), and the passive and introspective: "those quiet, anonymous individuals whose world is their mind, whose activity is contemplation, whose life is a quiet developing of their inner powers" ("jenen ruhigen, unbekannten Menschen, deren Welt ihr Gemüt, deren Tätigkeit die Betrachtung, deren Leben ein leises Bilden ihrer innern Kräfte ist" [I, 171]). The latter, Novalis states, are the poets, whom he characterizes as "men of passage," an epithet which suggests that he is thinking first of the wandering minstrels of Ofterdingen's day: "these rare men of passage who at times wander through our dwellings and everywhere revive mankind's old venerable worship and man's first gods—the stars, the spring, love, happiness, fertility, health and gaiety" ("diese seltenen Zugmenschen, die zuweilen durch unsere Wohnsitze wandeln, und überall den alten, ehrwürdigen Dienst der Menschheit und ihrer ersten Götter, der Gestirne, des Frühlings, der Liebe, des Glücks, der Fruchtbarkeit, der Gesundheit, und des Frohsinns erneuern" [I, 171f]). (It is revealing to see that what Novalis here suggests are the recurrent themes of poetry are embodied in the first song of the youth of the Atlantis fable.) Heinrich, Novalis continues, was born to be a poet. But, though his experiences have opened windows within him, as yet the soul of the world has not been revealed to him. The experience that is to transform Heinrich completely is anticipated in the words "A poet was already drawing near, a lovely girl at his hand, to open Heinrich's timid lips with sounds of his mother tongue and the touch of a sweet, gentle mouth, and to develop Heinrich's simple harmony into endless melodies" ("Schon nahte sich ein Dichter, ein liebliches Mädchen an der Hand, um durch Laute der Muttersprache und durch Berührung eines süssen zärtlichen Mundes, die blöden Lippen aufzuschliessen, und den einfachen Akkord in unendliche Melodien zu entfalten" [I, 172]). Like the youth of the Atlantis fable Heinrich is to have his lips unsealed by love and the spirit of poetry. With his journey to Augsburg completed, he meets the poet Klingsohr at his grandfather's home. In Klingsohr Heinrich recognizes the noble figure who had so often stood at his side in the illustrations of Hohenzollern's book. Gradually the various threads of the story to this point are pulled together. We see that the Atlantis fable relates directly to Heinrich's fate. Of Klingsohr's daughter Mathilde it is said: "She seemed the spirit of her father in the most lovely guise" ("Sie schien der Geist ihres Vaters in der lieblichsten Verkleidung" [I, 175]), while later Heinrich exclaims: "Oh, she is the visible spirit of song, a worthy daughter of her father" ("O! sie ist der sichtbare Geist des Gesanges, eine würdige Tochter ihres Vaters" [I, 181]). Thus metaphor equates Mathilde with the princess of the fable as the symbol of the poetic spirit. (There is a rather obvious similarity in that both Mathilde and the princess are motherless. In Novalis' notes we find direct identification of

Klingsohr with the king of the fable [I, 241].) Like the court of
the fable, the home of Heinrich's grandfather Schwaning is ruled
by the spirit of poetry, and its life, too, is one of blissful gaiety
and spirited happiness. Imagery forms an immediate bond between
the two levels of action. We are reminded of the images depicting
the splendid life of the court, the complete absence of chaotic and
disturbing influences, when Novalis characterizes the atmosphere
of Schwaning's household: "The enjoyment of life stood before
him [Heinrich] like a sounding tree laden with golden fruit.[1] Evil
was not to be seen, and it seemed to him impossible that mankind's
concern should ever have turned from this tree to the dangerous
fruit of knowledge, to the tree of war" ("Der Lebensgenuss stand
wie ein klingender Baum voll goldener Früchte vor ihm. Das
Übel liess sich nicht sehen, und es dünkte ihm unmöglich, dass je
die menschliche Neigung von diesem Baume zu der gefährlichen
Frucht des Erkenntnisses, zu dem Baume des Krieges sich ge-
wendet haben sollte" [I, 176]). Heinrich, falling in love with
Mathilde, is now able to put his emotions into words. The kiss
they exchange enables him to grasp the relationship of all that
has befallen him: "Do I not feel as I did in that dream as I caught
sight of the blue flower? What strange connection exists between
Mathilde and this flower? That face that inclined towards me
from the calyx was Mathilde's heavenly face, and now I remember
too having seen it in that book" ("Ist mir nicht zumute wie in
jenem Traume, beim Anblick der blauen Blume? Welcher sonderbare Zusammenhang ist zwischen Mathilden und dieser Blume?
Jenes Gesicht, das aus dem Kelche sich mir entgegenneigte, es war
Mathildens himmlisches Gesicht, und nun erinnere ich mich auch,
es in jenem Buche gesehn zu haben" [I, 181]). (There is a later,
implicit identification of Mathilde with the blue flower, through
color imagery, when Heinrich says: "Dear Mathilde, I should like
to call you a precious, pure sapphire. You are as clear and trans-
parent as the sky, you shine with the gentlest radiance"—"Liebe
Mathilde, ich möchte Euch einen köstlichen lautern Saphir nennen.
Ihr seid klar und durchsichtig wie der Himmel, Ihr erleuchtet mit

---

[1] This synaesthetic image conveys both the sensuous appeal of the new
world Heinrich has entered and the fact that life stands before him with
the promise of a tree laden with rich fruit ready to be plucked. The
subsequent metaphors, of course, develop from this image.

dem mildesten Lichte" [I, 184].) Love and the spirit of poetry personified in Mathilde have finally revealed to Heinrich the relationship of dream, book, and his experiences. The full significance of the blue flower has not yet been made known, but its relationship to Mathilde, and thence to the spirit of poetry, is now established.

In the same mood of excitement that accompanied his first dream, Heinrich dreams again. Once more the images of the dream presage his future life. Before his eyes Mathilde is drowned in a deep-blue river—the color blue again dominates the dream—and Heinrich, having plunged into the stream in a vain attempt at rescue, loses consciousness. He awakens in a region at first strange but then mysteriously familiar. There trees and flowers speak to him and soon he finds Mathilde. She tells him they are beneath the stream, "with our parents" (I, 182). As they embrace Mathilde tells him they will be together forever and speaks a strange word, "a wonderful, mysterious word . . . that resounded through his very being" (I, 183). Awakened, Heinrich cannot recall the word, which seemed to have such significance. For the moment, however, his happiness lets him forget the forebodings of the dream.

From this point until the narration of Klingsohr's "Märchen" the action of the novel is limited to further avowals of love by the young couple and to conversations between Klingsohr and Heinrich on the nature of poetry. The parallelism of the Atlantis fable and the action of the novel thus far is sufficiently striking to suggest that Heinrich's poetry is to be as different from that of Klingsohr as the song of the young naturalist was from the poetry of the court. Klingsohr's words do indeed reveal that his nature differs greatly from that of Heinrich. The latter has been shown to be naive and intuitive, receptive and impressionable, highly emotional and quick to enthusiasm. Klingsohr, on the other hand, is seen to be mature and sober, a man who regards not the heart but the intellect as the power that should guide man. His advice to Heinrich reveals a rather dispassionate and rationalistic approach to poetry: "I cannot commend to you enough the reinforcing with diligence and effort of your understanding, of your natural impulse to know how everything happens and how all things are interconnected through laws of causality . . . Inspiration without understanding is useless and dangerous, and the poet will be able to

perform few miracles if he is himself astonished at miracles . . .
The young poet cannot be detached or reflective enough . . . When
a torrent rages in your breast, all that comes forth is a confused
prattling" ("Ich kann Euch nicht genug anrühmen, Euren Verstand, Euren natürlichen Trieb, zu wissen, wie alles sich begibt
und untereinander nach Gesetzen der Folge zusammenhängt, mit
Fleiss und Mühe zu unterstützen . . . Begeisterung ohne Verstand
ist unnütz und gefährlich, und der Dichter wird wenig Wunder tun
können, wenn er selbst über Wunder erstaunt . . . Der junge
Dichter kann nicht kühl, nicht besonnen genug sein . . . Es wird
ein verworrnes Geschwätz, wenn ein reissender Strom in der Brust
tobt" [I, 184f]). For Klingsohr, poetry is above all an art form
demanding strict control and discipline: "Poetry must above all . . .
be practiced as a strict art" ("Die Poesie will vorzüglich . . . als
strenge Kunst getrieben werden" [I, 186]). In a later conversation
(Chapter VIII) Klingsohr, who has now invited Heinrich to
become his pupil, warns him that the poet must first know the limits
of both language and poetry and suggests that not the subject
matter of the art but the execution of form is of first concern to
the artist. Clearly, Klingsohr is representative of the artist who
emphasizes the rational element in creation and who subordinates
inspiration to the demands of form. There are two conclusions
to be drawn from the Atlantis fable. The one, that the poetry
represented by Klingsohr is, in Novalis' eyes, as far removed from
nature as was the court of Atlantis. The second, that Heinrich
will create a new poetry that will transcend Klingsohr's art—though
preserving what is best in it—as it unites the spirit of nature with
the spirit of traditional poetry. (There would seem to be every
good reason, judging from Klingsohr's words here quoted, for the
belief held by many critics that in Klingsohr Novalis has given us
his portrait of Goethe. These critics, however, regard the portrait
as an unqualified tribute to Goethe. They fail to draw the inference
that Novalis here subtly suggests that Romantic poetry will
transcend the poetry represented in his eyes by Goethe. The
portrait is, of course, by no means intended to be entirely dis-
paraging, but to show what Novalis regarded as definite failings
in Goethe's art.)

In these same conversations Klingsohr touches upon the theme
of the element in nature hostile to art, the theme of the Arion

fable that is revealed in implicit images throughout the fragment:
"I don't know ... why people regard it as poetry in the ordinary
sense when they call nature a poet. She isn't at all times. In
nature, as in man, there is a contradictory force—crude greed and
dull insensitivity and sluggishness that carry on a restless struggle
with poetry. It would make fine material for a poem, this mighty
struggle" ("Ich weiss nicht ... warum man es für Poesie nach
gemeiner Weise hält, wenn man die Natur für einen Poeten aus-
gibt. Sie ist es nicht zu allen Zeiten. Es ist in ihr, wie in dem
Menschen, ein entgegengesetztes Wesen, die dumpfe Begierde und
die stumpfe Gefühllosigkeit und Trägheit, die einen rastlosen Streit
mit der Poesie führen. Er wäre ein schöner Stoff zu einem Gedicht, dieser gewaltige Kampf" [I, 188]). Of this and of much
else in their conversations, Klingsohr tells Heinrich, the latter will
be reminded in the telling of the "Märchen" that Klingsohr composed when a young man. (There is, I believe, significance in the
fact that Klingsohr states, in somewhat of an apologetic tone, that
he composed the fable as a young man. The inference is that it
was created before he became the rationalist he now is and when
he was still guided by his heart and imagination rather than by his
precepts). With the telling of Klingsohr's fable, one of Novalis'
most delightful creations, we reach the climax of the first part of
Heinrich von Ofterdingen. Heinrich's apprenticeship is at an end.
When next we meet him, it is as a poet. Klingsohr's "Märchen"
stands, then, at the turning point of the action of the novel, a fact
which suggests that particular importance attaches to it. It is both
a bridge between the two halves of the work and, as I shall
endeavor to demonstrate, a symbolic presentation of the main
action of the completed novel as Novalis planned it.

CHAPTER VII

KLINGSOHR'S "MÄRCHEN"—*HEINRICH VON OFTERDINGEN (II)*

In Klingsohr's "Märchen" Novalis has presented us with a series of brilliantly colorful, rapidly flowing images and an apparent confusion of mythology. Figures from Greek and Nordic myth mingle with others of the poet's own creation. (This is presumably what Novalis called "the mixing of the romantic spirit of every age" when speaking of his fairy tale to Friedrich Schlegel [IV, 343].) Certain images have allusion to astrology and to the scientific theories of the poet's day, particularly to the ideas of Galvani. Other images—the phoenix, the marriage of king and queen, for example—would seem to derive from alchemical allegory, though the fable itself is not alchemical allegory. Jacob Böhme may have furnished Novalis with the figure of Sophie. In Böhme, Sophie is the mirror of God or the love of God, yet of one substance with God. However, either the Sophie who was Ofterdingen's patroness or Novalis' own fiancée may have provided him with the name for this symbolic figure. Finally, Goethe's *Märchen* may have had indirect influence, though the unequivocal proof of such influence would be difficult to establish. It is important, however, that we do not attach too much weight to the origins of the symbolic figures used by Novalis or to their original value as symbols. Many of the figures of the tale have more than one symbolic function. What their real significance is can be deduced only from the sphere of reference in which they move— the "Märchen" itself. In that there is no fixed system of symbols this tale is not pure allegory. It is rather a symbolic—and often humorous—action which hints at hidden meaning without presenting this meaning in consistently developed metaphor. Klingsohr had indicated to Heinrich that the fairy tale would remind him of much that had been said in their conversations and, indeed, one of its themes is the conflict between the spirit of poetry and the forces hostile to it. At the same time, it seems likely that the "Märchen" points forward to the action of the second part of the novel. Indeed, certain notes made by Novalis identify figures of the larger work with characters of the tale. Hence a detailed analysis of its imagery should present reasonably conclusive evidence for what Novalis planned as the action of the second part of his work.

The main action of the "Märchen" moves among three realms. We are first introduced to the upper realm, which at the beginning of the narrative is devoid of blooming life: "The long night had just begun . . . ornamental clay vessels filled with an endless variety of flowers of ice and snow . . . the garden, which consisted of metal trees and crystal plants and which was spangled with jewel-flowers and fruits . . . a high fountain in the middle of the garden, its waters frozen . . ." ("Die lange Nacht war eben angegangen . . . zierliche Gefässe von Ton, voll der mannigfaltigsten Eis- und Schneeblumen . . . der Garten . . ., der aus Metallbäumen und Kristallpflanzen bestand, und mit bunten Edelsteinblüten und Früchten übersäet war . . . einen hohen Springquell in der Mitte des Gartens, der zu Eis erstarrt war . . ." [I, 194]). This realm is thought of in one respect as the region of the North Pole, though it is at the same time the realm of the stars, ruled by King Arcturus in whose retinue follow the spirits of the constellations.[1] With his daughter Freya the king plays a card game, the cards bearing the symbols of the constellations. As the cards are placed on the table, the stars change positions and form new groupings: "At the same time there was heard in the air soft but deeply moving music that seemed to have its source in the stars intertwining strangely

---

[1] The idea of the Polar regions bursting into life in the new Golden Age is to be found elsewhere in Novalis. *Cf.* above, p. 81. Arcturus is the name of a giant fixed star in the northern constellation of Boötes. *Cf.* F. J. Obenauer, *Hölderlin-Novalis* (Jena, 1925), p. 252. Of a depiction of Arcturus at a later point in the fable Obenauer says: "This corresponds exactly to the pattern of the sky map in as much as above Arcturus is the Northern Crown, at his immediate right is Libra [the scales], below to the left is the constellation of Leo [the lion] and below to the right is the constellation of the Eagle" ("Dies entspricht insofern genau den Bildern der Sternkarte als über Arktur die nördliche Krone, rechts neben ihm das Sternbild der Wage steht, und dass weiter links unten das Tierkreisbild des Löwen, rechts unten das Sternbild des Adlers zu finden ist").

in the hall and in other remarkable movements" [2] ("Zugleich liess sich eine sanfte, aber tief bewegende Musik in der Luft hören, die von den im Saale sich wunderlich durch einander schlingenden Sternen und den übrigen sonderbaren Bewegungen zu entstehen schien" [I, 196]). Arcturus thus symbolizes the guiding spirit of the universe, a spirit that finds delight in harmony and order. Yet, at the same time, it is suggested that certain unalterable laws function independently of Arcturus: "At times he seemed compelled to select this or that particular card" ("Zuweilen schien er gezwungen zu sein, dies oder jenes Blatt zu wählen" [I, 196]).

Arcturus' kingdom embraces more than the astral bodies and the laws governing their courses, however. His daughter Freya, who as the personification of peace bears the title "der Friede," would seem also to represent the physical forces of the universe. From her body streams the only light that breaks the darkness of the long night. The light is created by the rubbing of her limbs as she lies on her throne formed from a sulphur crystal.[3] Warmth and electrical impulses that have an invigorating effect also proceed from her as she touches the shield of her retainer: "His armor resounded and a penetrating force animated his body. His eyes flashed and his heart pounded audibly against his armor" [4] ("Seine Rüstung klang, und eine durchdringende Kraft beseelte seinen Körper. Seine Augen blitzten und das Herz pochte hörbar an den Panzer" [I, 195]).

The third important figure in Arcturus' realm is this retainer. He is first identified as "the old hero" ("der alte Held"), but he also bears the names Iron and Perseus. Thus he too has a variety of symbolic qualities. As Iron he represents the prime element of the earth and certain magnetic forces. It is his signal, the striking of his sword on his shield, that brings the palace into activity at the beginning of the "Märchen," when it produces the first ray of light from Freya's body. His presence among Arcturus' retinue,

---

[2] A readily recognizable allusion to the familiar image of the harmony of the spheres.

[3] Novalis here has reference to the fact that electricity may be produced by rubbing sulphur crystals with other bodies. The light is, of course, the Aurora borealis, believed to be caused by electrical influences.

[4] This image would seem to allude to the theories of Galvani concerning the effects of electrical currents on muscular activity. In Novalis' day electricity was widely held to be the animating force of matter.

where we later find Zinc, Gold and Tourmaline, indicates that
Arcturus' realm also embraces the basic elements of the universe.
With the name Perseus, the name of a northern constellation, the
warrior also occupies a place among the stars: "The spirits of the
stars arranged themselves about the throne and the hero took his
place in their ranks" ("Die Geister der Gestirne stellten sich um
den Thron, und der Held nahm in der Reihe seinen Platz ein"
[I, 196]). The double designation of this figure suggests a link
between this realm and the subterranean wealth of the earth.
Indeed, it could be said that all the elements which make up
Arcturus' realm represent qualities normally hidden from man. It
is the old warrior's sword which the king orders hurled out into
the world to point the way to his daughter's resting place: "Iron,
throw out your sword into the world so that they may learn where
Peace reposes" ("Eisen, wirf du dein Schwert in die Welt, dass
sie erfahren, wo der Friede ruht" [I, 197]). The sword has
magnetic qualities. Splinters from it rain down up the earth, one
of them pointing Eros' way to Freya. She thus represents the
greatest known magnetic force, the North Pole. Again, however,
because of the different qualities represented by this figure, it is
suggested that peace has a magnetic quality, that to it man is
eventually drawn.

In all then, Arcturus' realm has a broad area of symbolic references. As the upper realm of the fairy tale it is a heaven, though
it might better be described as a Platonic realm of ideas. It is the
realm of cosmic laws, natural forces and basic elements. It is both
of the earth and yet apart from it—the realm of nature which is
concealed from man's eyes. At the opening of the fable this kingdom is held in thrall by some petrifying force, not as yet identified.
That this state is not to be perpetuated, however, is shown in the
song of the bird as the king first appears:

> Not long will the handsome stranger tarry.
> Warmth approaches, eternity begins.
> The Queen will waken from long dreams
> When land and sea dissolve in love's hot glow.
> The cold night will flee this scene
> Only when Fable wins back her old rights.
> In Freya's womb the world will be kindled
> And every yearning find its yearning.

(Nicht lange wird der schöne Fremde säumen.
Die Wärme naht, die Ewigkeit beginnt.
Die Königin erwacht aus langen Träumen,
Wenn Meer und Land in Liebesglut zerrinnt.
Die kalte Nacht wird diese Stätte räumen,
Wenn Fabel erst das alte Recht gewinnt.
In Freyas Schoss wird sich die Welt entzünden
Und jede Sehnsucht ihre Sehnsucht finden.)

The song holds the promise of an end to the long night when, like the Sleeping Beauty, the slumbering queen shall be awakened by her lover. But first, before this anticipated eternal bliss can be realized, poetry, "Fabel," must regain its old rights.

Occupying a middle ground in the tale is a second realm, the home of a family. Frequent reference to it as "home" ("zu Hause") would suggest that this is earth, the sphere of human attributes which the several members of the family symbolize. Masculine and feminine qualities are exemplified in the father and mother, who personify respectively the mind and the heart. Their child is Eros, the symbol as his name suggests of love. At this stage of the action he is still a baby. His nurse Ginnistan, at the same time the father's mistress, also bears the name Fantasy ("die Phantasie") and symbolizes both man's imaginative powers and memory. She furnishes the scribe with information from time to time and her diary contains a history of the family. (Novalis may have taken the name of this figure from Wieland's *Dchinnistan, oder auserlesene Feen- und Geistermärchen*, 1786-1789. Wieland uses the spelling Ginnistan as a variant in the preface. The name is Arabic in origin; thus we have further allusion to the Orient as the world of fantasy.) The child of Ginnistan and the father is Fabel, the spirit of poetry and the only figure in the fable who is able to enter all three realms. Within the household, though not a member of the family, is the father's scribe, "der Schreiber," who, with his lamp upon which Eros cannot bear to look, represents the uninspired, ultra-rationalistic spirit. (Here, as elsewhere in the tale, the lamp is representative of the "light" of the Enlightenment—rationalism. The three fates, the scribe's partners in evil, also have lamps. The sun, a favorite symbol of the Enlightenment, appears later in the "Märchen" as a similar representation of reason. It is the sun that the scribe and his followers regard as their guiding

power.) So devoid of emotion is the scribe that he must tickle
himself in order to laugh. At the same time he also represents
evil and strife in the world. He is hostile to all members of the
family, but so long as Eros and Fabel are present he remains in
a subordinate rôle, carrying out the directions of the father: "The
father . . . repeatedly had something to tell the scribe. The latter
listened attentively and when he had written it down he handed
the pages to a noble, god-like woman who was leaning against an
altar. On the altar stood a dark bowl of water into which she
gazed with a serene smile" ("Der Vater . . . hatte unaufhörlich
dem Schreiber etwas zu sagen. Dieser vernahm ihn genau, und
wenn er es aufgezeichnet hatte, reichte er die Blätter einer edlen,
göttergleichen Frau hin, die sich an einen Altar lehnte, auf welchem
eine dunkle Schale mit klarem Wasser stand, in welches sie mit
heiterm Lächeln blickte" [I, 197]). This noble, god-like woman
is Sophie. Like the scribe, she is not actually a member of the
family, though she lives within the family circle on intimate and
harmonious terms. Her position at the altar suggests that she is a
priestess to the family and she is indeed its guiding spirit—Fabel
refers to herself later as the godchild of Sophie. With the title
Wisdom ("die Weisheit") Sophie symbolizes the wisdom, spiritual
force and hidden secrets of the universe, as is further suggested
by the epithets used to characterize her in the passage quoted
above, her presence at the altar, and by the fact that she is a veiled
figure. (This last fact is suggested later in the story. In Novalis'
notes we find Sophie identified as "the sacred, the unknown"—
"das Heilige, Unbekannte" [I, 241].) On the altar stands the
bowl of liquid into which the pages written by the scribe are
plunged: "On each occasion she dipped the pages into the bowl.
When on drawing them out she perceived that some of the writing
remained and had taken on a lustrous glow she gave the page
back to the scribe, who fastened it in a large book and often
seemed vexed when his efforts were in vain and everything was
obliterated" ("Sie tauchte die Blätter jedesmal hinein, und wenn
sie beim Herausziehn gewahr wurde, dass einige Schrift stehen
geblieben und glänzend geworden war, so gab sie das Blatt dem
Schreiber zurück, der es in ein grosses Buch heftete, und oft ver-
driesslich zu sein schien, wenn seine Mühe vergeblich gewesen
und alles ausgelöscht war" [I, 197]). This liquid, we learn later,

is tears, though it would seem to symbolize truth, the implicit content of this last image being that the rationalistic spirit may only on occasion produce anything of true value. Later we see that all the pages written by Fabel pass the test. This great difference between the rationalistic and poetic spirits is further accentuated by the following delightful image: "At times the woman turned toward Ginnistan and the children, dipped her finger in the bowl and sprayed a few drops on them, which, as soon as they touched the nurse, one of the children, or the cradle, dissolved as a blue vapor that displayed a thousand curious pictures and circled about them constantly changing. If one of the drops by chance struck the scribe, a number of ciphers and geometric figures dropped down and these he drew with considerable eagerness upon a thread and hung them about his skinny neck as a piece of finery" ("Die Frau wandte sich zuzeiten gegen Ginnistan und die Kinder, tauchte den Finger in die Schale, und sprützte einige Tropfen auf sie hin, die, sobald sie die Amme, das Kind, oder die Wiege berührten, in einen blauen Dunst zerrannen, der tausend seltsame Bilder zeigte, und beständig um sie herzog und sich veränderte. Traf einer davon zufällig auf den Schreiber, so fielen eine Menge Zahlen und geometrische Figuren nieder, die er mit vieler Emsigkeit auf einen Faden zog, und sich zum Zierat um den magern Hals hing" [I, 197f]).

The action of the "Märchen" begins, essentially, with the father's discovery of an iron fragment, a splinter, we may assume, from Iron's sword which broke into fragments after flying through the air like a comet. The scribe readily determines the metal's magnetic qualities: "The scribe looked at it, turned it around with considerable delight, and soon established that, when suspended by a thread at its center, it turned automatically to the north" ("Der Schreiber besah es und drehte es mit vieler Lebhaftigkeit herum, und brachte bald heraus, dass es sich von selbst, in der Mitte an einen Faden aufgehängt, nach Norden drehe" [I, 198]). In the hands of Ginnistan, however, the fragment performs very differently: "Ginnistan took it in her hand too, bent it, squeezed it, breathed on it, and quickly gave it the form of a snake that suddenly bit its own tail" ("Ginnistan nahm es auch in die Hand, bog es, drückte es, hauchte es an, und hatte ihm bald die Gestalt einer Schlange gegeben, die sich nun plötzlich in den Schwanz biss" [I, 198]). Given life by

Ginnistan's powers, the snake forms a circle without beginning
or end, in alchemical allegory a traditional symbol of eternity.
(The same symbol is found in Goethe's *Märchen*. In relating this
symbol to the magnet Novalis again alludes to the concept that
electrical impulses are the life force of matter.) The rationalistic
spirit discovers only the physical properties of nature, but man's
imaginative powers give life to nature and reveal its hidden truths.
Such is the implicit content of this last image—again a pronounced
indictment of the spirit that had dominated Novalis' century.

It is the electrical forces inherent in the magnet that bring Eros
into active life, raising him to manhood before the eyes of the
family and preparing him for his search as it points northward.
Eros, guided by the fragment of Iron's sword, is to seek the sleeping Freya in the north. Sophie, ignoring the proposals of the scribe,
tells him to depart with Ginnistan at once. Fantasy, however,
proves to be an unreliable guide for love. Instead of leading Eros
to his goal, Ginnistan takes him to the court of her father, the
Moon, the ruler of weather and of dreams. A poem describes
their journey: "Upon dark paths Love traveled,/Glimpsed only by
the Moon ... And hastily drew Fantasy/Love over river and
land" ("Die Liebe ging auf dunkler Bahn/Vom Monde nur er-
blickt ... Und eilig zog die Phantasie/Sie über Strom und Land"
[I, 200]). At the court of King Moon—we gather from the poem
that his kingdom lies somewhere between the middle and upper
realms of the fable—his subjects, the weather phenomena, present
themselves, a scene Novalis depicts in a series of delightful personification images. Then the moon gives his daughter the key to his
treasure chamber so that she may provide a spectacle for Eros.
The treasure chamber furnishes a wealth of dream images that
embrace all aspects of existence: "countless castles in the air ...
a romantic land ... a shipwreck ... the horribly beautiful eruption
of a volcano ... a pair of lovers in the most tender embrace
beneath sheltering trees ... a dreadful battle ... a theater ... a
youthful corpse on a bier ... a lovely mother with her child at her
breast ..." ("unzählige Luftschlösser ... ein romantisches Land ...
einen Schiffbruch ... den schrecklich schönen Ausbruch eines
Vulkans ... ein liebendes Paar unter schattenden Bäumen in den
süssesten Liebkosungen ... eine fürchterliche Schlacht ... ein
Theater ... einen judgendlichen Leichnam auf der Bahre ... eine

liebliche Mutter mit dem Kinde an der Brust..." [I, 202f]).
Gradually the various images flow together into one great final
scene that depicts a battle between the forces of death and the
children of life: "With shocking savagery the army of ghosts tore
the frail limbs of the living" ("Mit unerhörten Grausamkeiten zer-
riss das Heer der Gespenster die zarten Glieder der Lebendigen"
[I, 203]). The children of life are consumed by the flames of a
towering funeral pyre, but from the ashes suddenly flows a milky-
blue stream that swallows up the legions of death and destroys all
horror. Heaven and earth flow together in harmonious accord.
On the waves of the stream floats a wondrous flower. Above
stretches a brilliant arch upon which sit godlike figures on splendid
thrones. At the topmost point of the arch sits Sophie, the bowl
from the altar in her hand. Beside her is a noble man with an oak
wreath about his brow and a palm branch of peace in his hand.
Upon a lily leaf that bends over the calyx of the flower sits Fabel
singing, while within the calyx Eros sees himself bending over a
sleeping maiden who holds him in her embrace. A smaller blossom
folds about them so that they seem to be transformed from the
waist down into one flower. This final dream image presages the
final scene of the fable. It points to the eventual union of Eros
and Freya and suggests the rôle of Fabel and Sophie in the
denouement.

Intoxicated by this vision and seduced by Ginnistan, Eros
forgets his task. The absence of love and fantasy provides the
scribe with the long awaited opportunity to impose his dominion
upon the household. Winning the servants over to his side, he puts
the father and mother in chains. He is unable to capture Fabel and
Sophie, however, even though he destroys the altar. This action
needs little amplification. Reason may be able to subjugate the
mind and heart in the absence of love and fantasy—and persuade
the masses of its rightful authority. Yet though it destroys the
symbols of spiritual values it cannot hold fast to truth and poetry.

Fabel flees by a stair leading down to the third realm of the
fable, a realm where natural phenomena are inverted: "Every
shape here was obscure. The air was like a monstrous shadow;
in the sky stood a black, radiant body... Light and shadow
seemed here to have exchanged rôles" ("Alle Figuren waren hier
dunkel. Die Luft war wie ein ungeheurer Schatten; am Himmel

stand ein schwarzer strahlender Körper... Licht und Schatten
schienen hier ihre Rollen vertauscht zu haben" [I, 204f]). The
imagery at once suggests a connection between this realm of shades
and the "long night" that holds Arcturus' kingdom in its grip.
Before the gate of this lower realm lies a sphinx, which, like the
sphinx of the Oedipus legend, poses questions to Fabel. Her
answers point to Novalis' conception of the nature of the poetic
spirit. Fabel, like the legendary Orpheus, says she seeks in this
realm what is her own—the right of poetry, one assumes, to spin
the myth of life. She comes from "old times" yet will always
remain a child—the spirit of poetry is as old as man himself yet
ever youthful, fresh and naive. The sphinx tells Fabel that Love
is with Fantasy, but Fabel's triumphant exclamation, "Sophie and
Love," tells us that Eros will eventually be freed from Ginnistan's
direction and will fulfill his proper rôle under the guidance of
Sophie. Within the gate guarded by the sphinx dwell three old
sisters. In his depiction of them at their spinning Novalis has been
faithful to the Greek myth of the three fates who spin, measure
and cut off the thread of man's destiny. The sisters set Fabel to
spinning in the hope that she will be destroyed at this dangerous
task, but as she spins she catches sight through an opening in the
rock above her head of the constellation of the Phoenix. This, the
symbol of rebirth, calls to her lips a song depicting the rebirth of
souls long dead and of one harmonious life to be enjoyed by all.
The life-giving power of her song brings into existence countless
points of light in the dark cave which almost petrify the fates with
fear. The lights are banished, however, by the appearance of the
scribe, a mandrake root in hand. (In folklore we meet the belief
that death overtakes the one who uproots the mandrake. It is
presumably as a symbol of death that the mandrake root appears
here.) It is now apparent that the scribe, the symbol of evil and
strife on earth, is in league with the fates, the powers of death. He
is delighted to see Fabel apparently a prisoner in the world of the
shades and with great glee he tells the sisters of the aid being given
their cause by the misguided Eros: "I wanted to bring you the
comforting news that Eros is restlessly flying around and will keep
your shears busily occupied. His mother, who so often compelled
you to spin the threads longer, tomorrow falls victim to the flames"
("Ich wollte euch zu euerm Troste sagen, dass Eros ohne Rast

umherfliegt, und eure Schere fleissig beschäftigen wird. Seine
Mutter, die euch so oft zwang, die Fäden länger zu spinnen, wird
morgen ein Raub der Flammen" [I, 207]). The mother—the heart
from which flows the sympathy, kindness and affection that often
prolong human life—is to be destroyed by the scribe and his
followers.

Fabel is sent out by the fates to provide them with tarantulas
for oil for their lamps. (The lamps further suggest the complicity
of the sisters and the scribe, while the tarantulas, returning later
in the story, would seem to symbolize irrational passions.) Instead,
Fabel climbs the ladder leading to Arcturus' realm. With her
prophetic gifts Fabel is able to proclaim an early end to the long
night that still holds the palace in its power: "Glad tidings to your
wounded heart! Wisdom's early return! An eternal awakening
for Peace! Calm for restless Love! Transfiguration of the Heart!
Life for antiquity and form for the future!" ("frohe Botschaft deinem verwundeten Herzen! baldige Rückkehr der Weisheit! Ewiges
Erwachen dem Frieden! Ruhe der rastlosen Liebe! Verklärung
des Herzens! Leben dem Altertum und Gestalt der Zukunft!"
[I, 207f]). These words foretell the dawn of an eternal Golden
Age when man will have knowledge of both past and future, when
Arcturus shall be reunited with Sophie, "Wisdom." Then, too,
Freya shall be awakened by Eros who shall have ceased his restless
wanderings. Anticipated also is the transfiguration of the mother,
"the Heart." Fabel's last words before she asks for the lyre, the
symbol of her powers, tells of the early appearance of Eros at the
court. (The king takes the lyre from the "waters" of Eridanus.
The name is that of a southern constellation but is used here,
presumably, for the Milky Way, the river of stars.)

From her mother, Ginnistan, Fabel learns that Eros has again
been transformed as a result of the passions unleashed in him by
Ginnistan's caresses. Now in Cupid form he roams the earth
wreaking havoc with his arrows, a personified pagan love that is
without spiritual content. It is from this activity that the scribe
and the fates are able to draw consolation. Fabel's song, however, calms Eros and puts him to sleep. Then, from afar, Fabel
catches sight of the flames rising from the funeral pyre of Eros'
mother, but she is reassured by the vision of Sophie's blue veil
floating over the grave-like earth, an image which would suggest

the blue sky that conceals heaven from man's eyes while its beauty assures him of heaven's existence. As the flame rises and moves northward it absorbs the light of the sun, which falls as a black, lifeless disc into the sea, bringing fear to the scribe and his followers. Fabel enters the ruins of her home—the earth has become desolate under reason's rule. She is attacked by the scribe and his followers, but they are caught in the webs of tarantulas called into life by Fabel's song. As Fabel again descends into the lower realm, the completion of her task is now forecast in her exchange with the sphinx: "The sphinx asked, 'What is more sudden than lightning?' 'Revenge,' said Fabel. 'What is most transitory?' 'Unlawful possession.' 'Who knows the world?' 'He who knows himself.' 'What is the eternal secret?' 'Love.' 'Where is it to be found?' 'With Sophie' " ("Die Sphinx fragte: 'Was kommt plötzlicher, als der Blitz?'—'Die Rache,' sagte Fabel.— 'Was ist am vergänglichsten?'—'Unrechter Besitz.'—'Wer kennt die Welt?'—'Wer sich selbst kennt.'—'Was ist das ewige Geheimnis?'—'Die Liebe.'—'Bei wem ruht es?'—'Bei Sophien' " [I, 211]). Revenge, faster than lightning, has overtaken the scribe, whose illegitimate dominion of the household was but brief. The eternal secret of life is love, love that now recognizes its true nature under the sway of wisdom, for Eros, calmed by Fabel's song, has now rejoined Sophie. It remains now for Fabel to destroy the power of the fates. This she does by furnishing them with dresses adorned with flowers grown in the flame from the pyre—symbols of the new life that is victorious over death. At Arcturus' palace Fabel discovers that the life-bringing flame from the pyre has reached his kingdom; Arcturus proclaims: "The night is done and the ice is melting. My spouse reveals herself from afar. My enemy is consumed by flame. Everything is beginning to live. I may not let myself be seen yet, for alone I am not king" ("Die Nacht ist vorbei und das Eis schmilzt. Meine Gattin zeigt sich von weitem. Meine Feindin ist versengt. Alles fängt zu leben an. Noch darf ich mich nicht sehn lassen, denn allein bin ich nicht König" [I, 212]). The king envisions the advent of Sophie, his queen, without whose presence his power as ruler of the universe is nugatory. The enemy of whom he speaks is the sun (burned by the flame), the symbol of time and the spirit of rationalism that must be destroyed before the eternal Golden Age can begin. With the aid of the old hero, whose shield attracts to it the shears with which the fates cut off man's life, Fabel completes her victory over the forces of death and rises for the third time to Arcturus' realm. (The mythological slaying of the Medusa, a victory comparable to that of Fabel, may have suggested to Novalis the name Perseus for his warrior.) To the king Fabel proclaims the final victory of the powers of life: "The flax is all used up. The forces of death are rendered powerless. The powers of life shall rule and shall form and use that which was without life" ("Der Flachs ist versponnen. Das Leblose ist wieder entseelt. Das Lebendige wird regieren, und das Leblose bilden und gebrauchen" [I, 213]). She asks for the aid of Zinc, Tourmaline and Gold in performing two final tasks: "I must gather up the ashes of my foster mother, and old Atlas must be resurrected so that the earth may soar again and not lie upon chaos" ("Die Asche meiner Pflegemutter muss ich sammeln, und der alte Träger muss wieder aufstehn, dass die Erde wieder schwebe und nicht auf dem Chaos liege" [I, 213]). At the other side of the earth, Fabel and her companions find the old giant, lamed and paralyzed. The imagery at this point is surprisingly logical. Pictures of Atlas supporting the earth invariably depict the region of the world resting on his shoulders as the South Pole—the other side of the world from Arcturus' realm. Myth in the person of Atlas, robbed of its vitality by the rationalistic spirit and the death-horror, is to be revived by the victorious spirit of poetry and the sciences. Once again Novalis depicts the creation of an electrical current that serves as an animating force: "Gold put a coin in Atlas' mouth and the flower gardner [Zinc] placed a dish below his loins. Fabel touched his eyes and emptied the vessel over his brow. As the water flowed over his eyes into his mouth and down over him into the dish, a flash of life made every muscle twitch. He opened his eyes and raised himself up vigorously" ("Gold legte ihm eine Münze in den Mund, und der Blumengärtner [Zink] schob eine Schüssel unter seine Lenden. Fabel berührte ihm die Augen und goss das Gefäss auf seiner Stirn aus. Sowie das Wasser über das Auge in den Mund und herunter über ihn in die Schüssel floss, zuckte ein Blitz des Lebens ihm in allen Muskeln. Er schlug die Augen auf und hob sich rüstig empor" [I, 213f]).

At home Fabel finds Sophie at the rebuilt altar with a chastened and serious Eros at her feet. As Fabel hands the ashes to Sophie, the latter tells her: "Dear child ... your faith and zeal have won for you a place among the eternal stars. You chose the immortal part of your being. The phoenix is yours. You will be the spirit of our life. Now awaken the bridegroom. The herald calls, and Eros is to seek Freya and rouse her from her sleep" ("Liebliches Kind ... dein Eifer und deine Treue haben dir einen Platz unter den ewigen Sternen erworben. Du hast das Unsterbliche in dir gewählt. Der Phönix gehört dir. Du wirst die Seele unsers Lebens sein. Jetzt wecke den Bräutigam auf. Der Herold ruft, und Eros soll Freya suchen und aufwecken" [I, 214]). Fabel's victory over the powers of death have won for her the phoenix, the symbol of a life that emerges from apparent death and here representative of the power of poetry to give life to the dead past. Now, before Eros departs to find Freya, the father, soon to be the bridegroom of Ginnistan, is awakened from the sleep into which he had fallen while a prisoner of the scribe. (This image suggests that the mind is eventually paralyzed when reason assumes full direction of the faculties.) The metals again combine their inherent powers to produce an electrical current. The chain and golden coin used to create the current melt together to form a mirror, which Sophie says will reflect everything in its true image, destroy every illusion and hold fast the original image—the symbol, one might assume, of a single, synthesized science that is to reveal truth to man on earth. (On this occasion Novalis may have reference to the al-chemical experiments of obtaining gold from base metals, so adapted as to depict the elimination of all base qualities from the father, leaving only the pure.) Novalis, it would seem, envisioned the emergence of a new scientific spirit, divorced from rational thought processes and guided by the spirit of poetry. This new, synthesized science, it might be inferred, would be able to lead man to ultimate truth.

The ashes of the mother are mixed with the water on the altar and each member of the family takes and drinks of the body of the mother, now transfigured as Fabel had foretold: "All of them sipped the divine drink and with inexpressible joy perceived within them the salutation of the mother. She was manifested to each of them, and her mysterious presence seemed to transfigure every-body ... Sophie said, 'The great secret is revealed to all and yet remains forever unfathomable. The new world is born of pain, and the ashes are dissolved in tears as the drink of life eternal. In everyone dwells the divine mother to bear eternally every child' " ("Alle kosteten den göttlichen Trank, und vernahmen die freundliche Begrüssung der Mutter in ihrem Innern, mit unsäglicher Freude. Sie war jedem gegenwärtig, und ihre geheimnisvolle Anwesenheit schien alle zu verklären ... Sophie sagte: 'Das grosse Geheimnis ist allen offenbart, und bleibt ewig unergründlich. Aus Schmerzen wird die neue Welt geboren, und in Tränen wird die Asche zum Trank des ewigen Lebens aufgelöst. In jedem wohnt die himmlische Mutter, um jedes Kind ewig zu gebären' " [I, 215]). In this image the act of Communion is adapted to the symbolism of the "Märchen." I shall reserve discussion of it until later, when I examine the rôle of Eros.

Eros and Fabel depart on their journey to awaken Freya, finding as they go a new Eden in a world enjoying a new spring. Life is everywhere bursting forth. Dust is assuming the shape of living creatures, while animals converse with a revitalized mankind. At the edge of the sea, the pair find a steel boat which carries them northward as it is drawn on by magnetic force, finally to reach the palace of Arcturus. A flash of electricity from Eros to Freya awakens the slumbering maiden and the two seal their eternal bond with a kiss. The king enters with Sophie, followed by the stars and the spirits of nature. The astral world and the ideal nature realm are rejoined in the reunion of king and queen. Eros and Freya are crowned the new royal pair and are hailed by the people, who recognize them as their rulers in a former time. A new light to replace the vanquished sun is created as Freya, at Sophie's command, hurls her bracelet through the air: "The bracelet dissolved in the air and soon bright halos were to be seen about every head; a brilliant band of light stretched over city, sea and earth, and the earth celebrated an everlasting festival of spring" ("Das Armband zerfloss in der Luft, und bald sah man lichte Ringe um jedes Haupt, und ein glänzendes Band zog sich über die Stadt und das Meer und die Erde, die ein ewiges Fest des Frühlings feierte" [I, 217]). Perseus presents Eros with a chessboard—"the remains of your enemies"—a symbol of the end of strife and hatred and, perhaps, of harmless reason as a game. Fabel receives the spindle of the fates as she hovers above the

throne on the wings of the phoenix. Now, with the forces of death banished, poetry creates a new myth of life: "She sang a wondrous song and began to spin, while the thread seemed to unreel from her breast" ("Sie sang ein himmlisches Lied, und fing zu spinnen an, indem der Faden aus ihrer Brust sich hervorzuwinden schien" [I, 217f]). The moon and his subjects join the company, as do the father and Ginnistan, now created viceroys of Eros and Freya on earth. The arrival of the Hesperides, whose golden fruit and wondrous garden characterize the richness of life in the new age, accompanies the transformation of the throne into a bridal bed: "The king embraced his blushing beloved, and the people followed their king's example, caressing one another" ("Der König umarmte seine errötende Geliebte, und das Volk folgte dem Beispiel des Königs, und liebkoste sich untereinander" [I, 218]). The new Golden Age has begun and the "Märchen" ends with Fabel's song:

> Established is the realm of eternity,
> The struggle ends in love and peace;
> Ended is the long dream of pain,
> Sophie is forever priestess of our hearts.

> (Gegründet ist das Reich der Ewigkeit,
> In Lieb' und Frieden endigt sich der Streit,
> Vorüber ging der lange Traum der Schmerzen,
> Sophie ist ewig Priesterin der Herzen.)

Klingsohr's "Märchen" is one of the most remarkable creations in German literature, a tale of prodigious scope. While far removed from popular fairy tale in the nature of its theme and imagery, it retains much of the naive tone and spirit of that genre. Though its theme is a serious one, it has many amusing moments. With its fascinating characters, rapid changes of scene, and brilliant color, it continues to appeal after repeated reading. This lasting attraction is due in large measure to Novalis' avoidance of pure allegory as his mode of presentation. While the "Märchen" is largely allegoric, its imagery and symbolic figures have relatively broad areas of reference. Certainly Novalis has given us far more explicit indication of the particular values of his symbols than did Goethe in his *Märchen*. Most of the figures in Klingsohr's tale are designated, for example, by specific epithet as well as by name. At the same time, however, as I have earlier remarked, these figures have often more than one symbolic function. Despite its allegoric nature, then, there attaches to the "Märchen" a quality of indefiniteness in certain of its elements. It is a quality that was doubtless intended. Yet its position within the novel, the similarity of certain of its images to images in the larger work, and Novalis' identification in his notes of figures in the tale with characters in the novel itself indicate that a meaningful interpretation can result only from an analysis of its content in relationship to the larger context. Indeed, the main action of the "Märchen" is anticipated, I suggest, in the novel's recurrent image of the conflict between the poetic spirit and the forces that oppose it. Moreover, we find a virtual statement of the tale's theme in the first song of the youth of the legend of Atlantis: "It dealt with the origins of the world, of the stars, plants, animals and man, with the almighty sympathy of nature, with the ancient Golden Age and its rulers, Love and Poetry, with the appearance of hatred and barbarism and their struggles against those benevolent goddesses, and finally the song told of the future triumph of the latter, of the end of misery, the rejuvenation of nature and the return of an eternal Golden Age" (I, 130).

In this song and in Klingsohr's "Märchen" Novalis presents us with an imaginatively conceived mythological world picture. Like the fifth Hymn to the Night, this treats of three great phases of human culture. The first is an original Golden Age when men worshiped spiritual powers symbolized in the stars or in the figures of their mythology, gods personifying the forces that ruled the world. The second period is an age of barbarism, strife and fear, when men lost faith in myth and sought to control their destiny by the power of their intellect. The third period sees a return of the Golden Age when the hostile forces of the middle period have been destroyed and the spiritual values restored. In the "Märchen" the first period has already ended as the narration begins. The "long night," the middle period in which the action takes place, has begun. (That a Golden Age had gone before, however, is made plain later in the narrative.) Arcturus' kingdom, the spiritual realm, a heaven or a Platonic realm of ideas, is held in thrall by the forces hostile to it. Only gradually are these revealed as the power of death over life and its manifestation on earth as evil, hatred, strife, and rationalism. The fifth Hymn to the Night shows that it was the failure of myth to explain the true nature of death that had caused mankind to lose its original faith and to turn its back on its gods. With the loss of this faith the Golden Age was ended. Gone were the naive bliss and intimate knowledge of nature that men had enjoyed. This same idea is suggested by the imagery of Klingsohr's tale. The main action of the novel is concerned with the struggle of the powers of life and the powers of death. The apparent victory of death over life must be reversed in order that a new Golden Age may come into being. Then, as spiritual values regain their rightful place in the universe, the rulers in the former Golden Age may crown the new rulers, love and peace. Peace has fled the earth, to take refuge in Arcturus' realm while the hostile forces hold sway on earth. She can be roused from her slumber only by love. The task of securing the victory for the forces of life and of preparing the advent of the Golden Age falls to poetry, to Fabel. Yet Fabel does not represent the myth of the former Golden Age. That myth, personified in the figure of Atlas, has been paralyzed. She personifies a new poetic spirit that draws its inspiration from the spiritual realm—Fabel directed by Sophie and armed with the lyre from Arcturus' hands. This new poetic spirit, while it revives those elements of the myth that had given meaning to life in the Golden Age and had brought man close to his gods, transcends that older poetic spirit. It is able to destroy that aspect of the old myth that persuaded man of the power of death over life, symbolized by the fates. Only after the destruction of the fates can the union of Eros and Freya be realized. Only then can love and peace rule over the new Golden Age. But love itself must first be purified before it can play its part. Eros, it will be remembered, grew to full stature only under the influence of the spiritual realm (represented in the action of the "Märchen" by his growth from a baby to manhood after touching the magnetic splinter that pointed the way to Freya). But his first transformation made of him only the personification of pagan love—Eros in Cupid form after his seduction by Gin-nistan. Such love that knows only erotic passion cannot restore the Golden Age and bring back peace to the world. Love in this form, the action shows, only aids the fates and their ally the scribe, the personification of strife and rationalism. It is a chastened Eros, a love again transformed, that finally discovers Freya. The full development of Eros is one of the most significant elements of the tale, vital to our understanding of Novalis' purpose. The symbolic value of the purified Eros is revealed through the images of the flame from the funeral pyre and the drinking of the water mixed with the ashes of the mother. The flame, like the milky-blue stream of the dream sequence (the two are surely one and the same), symbolizes the victory of life over death. It is the flame that destroys the sun, the symbol of time and of the apparent power of death over life. The flame, too, consumes the darkness of the long night, brings back life to Arcturus' kingdom, and ultimately furnishes Fabel with the weapons that destroy the fates—flowers grown in its radiance. In its wake life everywhere blossoms forth in a new springtime. From the ashes of the body that gave birth to the flame, the ashes of the mother, all draw new life and strength in the Communion-like act that is the last scene on earth in the fable. The mother, the symbol of the life-force and the eternal act of rebirth, is virtually equated by Novalis with the Virgin as Sophie calls her "the divine mother" ("die himmlische Mutter"). It is her death and transfiguration that completes the transformation of Eros. This transfiguration and the act of the living in drawing life from the dead is the "eternal secret" of which Sophie speaks. These images combine to suggest inevitably that the purified Eros symbolizes the love of Christ as well as erotic love. He is the personification of love both human and divine, love that reveals to man that death is but the gateway to an eternal life of love. The death and transfiguration of the mother creates a new Eros just as Christ's death and transfiguration created a new concept of love. Only this love can bring back peace and usher in the new Golden Age, for it alone reveals the true nature of death.[5] Poetry, too, partakes of

[5] The eventual identification of Eros with the love of Christ is anticipated, I believe, in the imagery of the first paragraph of the tale: "The entire scene was now visible, and the reflection of the figures, the bustle of spears, swords, shields and helmets which bowed from all sides to the crowns appearing here and there and which finally, as the crowns disappeared and gave way to a simple green wreath, formed a broad circle about the wreath—all this was mirrored in the frozen sea . . ." ("Die ganze Gegend ward nun sichtbar, und der Widerschein der Figuren, das Getümmel der Spiesse, der Schwerter, der Schilder und der Helme, die sich nach hier

this new life, and thus love, peace, and poetry regain their "old rights" in the new age. As Fabel's song at the end of the "Märchen" proclaims, the long dream of pain—the "unreal" existence of the middle period—is over and the struggle ends in the union of love and peace. When the people hail their old rulers who have always dwelt among them unrecognized, they acknowledge the restoration of the rightful order of the universe. Spiritual values and the forces of life have triumphed over the powers that sought to wrest away their authority, even as Fabel had predicted: "The forces of death are rendered powerless. The powers of life shall rule and shall form and use that which was without life" ("Das Leblose ist wieder entseelt. Das Lebendige wird regieren, und das Leblose bilden und gebrauchen" [I, 213]). The death-horror has been ended. The allies on earth of the powers of death have been rendered harmless. In their place, as viceroys of love and peace, the purified mind and fantasy are to reveal to man divine truth. Poetry creates a new myth of life that holds the promise of an eternal life of love and happiness in an everlasting springtime.

The content of this tale has obvious implications for Novalis' own day. Novalis clearly imagined his age as a "middle period," an age of irreligious speculation and materialism, a time when man sought to control his destiny and interpret the universe through his powers of reason. (Fabel's victory over the scribe would suggest the anticipated victory of the Romantic spirit over the spirit of the Enlightenment. The rôle of Eros indicates a belief in the eventual triumph of Christianity over atheism, while Freya's awakening envisions the return of peace to a war-torn Europe.) Such a restricted interpretation, however, would fail to do full justice to the work. Novalis' vision has a more universal application. His "Märchen" is the metaphorical representation of man's attainment to knowledge of the transcendent and the mysteries of life and death through the revealing powers of love and poetry. His presentation is poetic rather than ratiocinative. It persuades by virtue of its brilliant imagery rather than by reasoned argument. Novalis'

und da erscheinenden Kronen von allen Seiten neigten, und endlich wie diese verschwanden, und einem schlichten, grünen Kranze Platz machten, um diesen her einen weiten Kreis schlossen: alles dies spiegelte sich in dem starren Meere..." [I, 194]).

"Märchen" is a cosmic myth, yet the immediate import of its content is for the individual. Through the renunciation of rationalism and the belief in the finality of death, and through full acceptance of the poet's own irrational belief in the powers of love and poetry, the tale implies, the individual can regain the Golden Age for himself.

Klingsohr's "Märchen" is, as I have earlier pointed out, incontrovertibly linked to the larger work in its theme and its imagery. I shall reserve for later discussion its relationship to the projected second part of the novel, but at this point the links between the fable and other elements of "Die Erwartung" may be noted. We find the same theme of an eternal Golden Age in a land of everlasting springtime in the legend of Atlantis. Other parallels between the two tales are immediately apparent. In both, love is the key to the final resolution. Fabel's revival of Atlas, the transformation of Eros, and other elements in Klingsohr's "Märchen" suggest the combining of the best aspect of ancient myth with the new poetic spirit. Such a marriage of old and new is represented in the Atlantis story by the union of youth and princess. The conflict of the poetic spirit with the forces opposed to it in Klingsohr's tale is foreshadowed in the Arion episode. The concept of past and future united, to which there is frequent allusion in the "Märchen," is seen earlier in Heinrich's vision of the cathedral. The spiral image, to which attention has earlier been drawn, itself suggests a return to a state both old and new that is inherent in the concept of a Golden Age returned. Finally, the image in Eros' dream vision of a flower floating on the blue stream forces us to associate it with the blue flower that is the dominant symbol of the novel. Though the color of the flower is not explicitly stated, the color imagery forms a sufficiently strong bond. It is clear, then, that Klingsohr's "Märchen" is not an isolated element in the novel but a vital part of the total presentation that cannot be torn from its context if its full significance is to be appreciated.

CHAPTER VIII

"DIE ERFÜLLUNG"—*HEINRICH VON OFTERDINGEN (III)*

Among the many notes made by Novalis that clearly have reference to *Heinrich von Ofterdingen* are some which suggest the tremendous scope of the projected action of the second part. Since but little of "Die Erfüllung" was completed, however, we can only conjecture what its action was to have been. As the second book begins we learn early that the forebodings of Heinrich's second dream have been realized. Mathilde has been drowned. We must assume that Heinrich has been wandering from place to place, distracted by his loss. At the beginning of "Die Erfüllung" stands a poem with the title "Astralis." It serves both as a prologue and to identify the figure of Astralis. His name suggests at once that he is not of this earth but that he moves in the spiritual realm, a fact later made plain in the body of the poem. The first part of the poem alludes to his conception: "On a summer morning my young life began;/I felt then my own life's pulse/For the first time. And as love/Lost itself in more profound rapture/I wakened more and more ..." ("An einem Sommermorgen ward ich jung;/Da fühlt' ich meines eignen Lebens Puls/Zum erstenmal—und wie die Liebe sich/In tiefere Entzückungen verlor,/Erwacht' ich immer mehr ..." [I, 221]). Passion, Astralis says, was the procreative power of his existence. He is the symbol of the point in which yearnings are united with each other. Gradually his identity is revealed: "You know me not and yet saw my beginning./Did you not witness how I,/Sleepwalker still, met myself for the first time/On that happy evening?" ("Ihr kennt mich nicht und saht mich werden/Wart ihr nicht Zeugen, wie ich noch/Nachtwandler mich zum ersten Male traf/An jenem frohen Abend?"). His relationship to the blue flower is suggested by the delicate imagery in which he depicts the moment of his conception: "I lay completely wrapped in calyxes of honey flowers./I spread my fragrance, the flower gently swayed/In the golden air of dawn. An inner welling/I was, a soft struggling; everything flowed/Through me and over me and softly raised me./Then the first grain of pollen sank into the stigma,/Think of the kiss after they had left the table" ("Versunken lag ich ganz in Honigkelchen./Ich duftete, die Blume schwankte still/In goldner Morgenluft. Ein innres Quellen/War ich, ein sanftes Ringen, alles floss/Durch mich und über mich und hob mich leise./Da sank das erste Stäubchen in die Narbe,/Denkt an den Kuss nach aufgehobnem Tisch"). We recognize now in Astralis the child of Heinrich and Mathilde, conceived at their first kiss and given life by the mounting passion of his parents: "No longer merely individuals, Heinrich and Mathilde/Were joined in one image" ("Nicht einzeln mehr nur Heinrich und Mathilde/Vereinten beide sich zu einem Bilde"). The child grew toward the hour of his birth. Yet scarcely had he reached his final form as a living creature when Mathilde died, ending the physical existence of the child that had not known life independently of her: "New-born I soared towards heaven,/Consummated was my earthly destiny/In the blissful moment of transfiguration . . ." ("Ich hob mich nun gen Himmel neugeboren,/Vollendet war das irdische Geschick/Im seligen Verklärungsaugenblick . . .").

Astralis, the spiritual child of Heinrich and Mathilde, is the symbol of the new poetic spirit as was the child of the youth and princess of the Atlantis fable. (This interpretation is supported by Novalis' notes: "Birth of the sidereal being at the first embrace of Mathilde and Heinrich. This being now speaks between the chapters . . . Between each chapter speaks Poetry"—"Geburt des siderischen Menschen mit der ersten Umarmung Mathildens und Heinrichs. Dieses Wesen spricht nun immer zwischen den Kapiteln . . . Zwischen jedem Kapitel spricht die Poesie" [I, 240f].) His "birth" has heralded the birth of a new world which is the realm of action of "Die Erfüllung." This realm is depicted in the continuing verses of the poem as a realm of poetry, where past and future are united, where the familiar is strange and wonderful, and where the sympathy between all things is apparent. The imagery suggests that the action of the novel now moves in the world of Klingsohr's "Märchen": "The realm of love is opened,/Fable begins to spin" ("Der Liebe Reich ist aufgetan,/Die Fabel fängt zu spinnen an"). At the same time it would seem that the action of "Die Erfüllung" is to parallel in some measure the action of the fable. It will be recalled that Ginnistan, "Fantasy," first guided Eros, eventually showing him the dream vision. Accordingly, in this poem we find the verses: "Free shall fantasy first hold sway,/ Weaving the threads as she may please,/Veiling much here, revealing much there,/And finally floating off into a magic vapor" ("Frei soll die Phantasie erst schalten,/Nach ihrem Gefallen die Fäden verweben,/Hier manches verschleiern, dort manches entfalten/Und endlich in magischen Dunst verschweben"). The images of the closing verses suggest a transfiguration of Mathilde comparable to that of the mother in the "Märchen": "The body is dissolved in tears,/The world becomes a vast grave/Into which, consumed by fearful yearning,/The heart falls as ashes" ("Der Leib wird aufgelöst in Tränen,/Zum weiten Grabe wird die Welt,/ In das, verzehrt von bangem Sehnen,/Das Herz, als Asche, niederfällt").

The action of "Die Erfüllung" begins with the appearance of Heinrich, garbed as a pilgrim. Fear and despair have driven him to seek solitude in the mountains. His surroundings gradually soothe him. The forest and mountain seem to speak of the river that had taken Mathilde from him: "Hasten on then, river, you shall not escape us . . . Trust us, pilgrim, he is our enemy too, whom we ourselves created. Let him hasten off with his victim, he will not escape us" ("Eile nur, Strom, du entfliehst uns nicht . . . Vertraue du uns, Pilgrim, es ist auch unser Feind, den wir selbst erzeugten—Lass ihn eilen mit seinem Raub, er entflieht uns nicht" [I, 224]). The flowing stream seems to symbolize the transitory nature of human life, while it is from the unchanging forest and mountain that Heinrich draws comfort. From a tree above a great rock which Heinrich first believes is the old chaplain from his home (an allusion again to the existence of all things in one another), comes a song of the love of a mother for her child. Then, through the silence that follows, Heinrich hears the voice of Mathilde. She tells him that if he plays a song on his lute a girl will appear: "Take her with you and do not let her leave your side" (I, 225). Mathilde exhorts him to remember her when he comes to the Emperor and tells him that she has chosen this place to be with her child: "My child has conquered death . . . I am with you. You will remain yet a while on earth, but the girl will comfort you until you too die and enter into our life of joy" (I, 225f). Then, in a ray of light that penetrates through the branches of the tree from which the voice had come, Heinrich is given a vision of the realm beyond death. In the foreground stands Mathilde as though she would speak to him. His peace restored by the vision, Heinrich now understands that death is a revelation of life that makes the world more meaningful. (This vision is strikingly similar to the vision of the true nature of death depicted in the *Hymnen an die Nacht*. The similarity extends to both the nature of the vision and its effect upon the individual. We may infer from this image, I think, a belief on Novalis' part that every poet must have this revelation of death as a source of life. Like Fabel, every poet must descend into the realm of the shades in order that the real meaning of life itself may be understood.)

For the first time we see Heinrich as a poet as he sings a song dedicating the place of his vision as a shrine. When he has ended, a young girl, Cyane, appears before him. In Cyane, who has died and been reborn, it would seem that the spirit of Mathilde returns to guide Heinrich. Her words suggest that Mathilde, whose child has conquered death, is now equated in symbol with the Virgin, the mother of all: " 'Who told you about me?' asked the pilgrim. 'Our mother.' 'Who is your mother?' 'The mother of God' " (" 'Wer hat dir von mir gesagt?' frug der Pilgrim. 'Unsre Mutter.' —'Wer ist deine Mutter?'—'Die Mutter Gottes' " [I, 228]). This equating of Mathilde and the Virgin in a universal mother symbol may be anticipated in the words of Heinrich's song: "Mother of God and Beloved,/ ... Eternal Goodness, eternal Kindness,/Oh, I know, you are Mathilde/And the goal of all my thoughts" ("Gottes Mutter und Geliebte/ ... Ewge Güte, ewge Milde,/O! ich weiss, du bist Mathilde/Und das Ziel von meinem Sinnen" [I, 228]). (This may be compared with the equating of the mother of the fable with the Virgin.) A similar universal father image is created as Cyane states that Hohenzollern is both her father and Heinrich's. Again, her reference to the fact that her earthly mother, too, had told her of Heinrich and her words "You have more parents" lend further support to the belief that in Heinrich we have the universal image of the poet. Her reply to Heinrich's question as to their goal gives the spiral image its most pronounced expression: "Ever homeward" ("Immer nach Hause" [I, 229]).

Led by Cyane to the ruins of an old monastery, Heinrich finds there an old man, Sylvester, whose life is devoted to the study of nature. Heinrich believes he recognizes in Sylvester the miner of his earlier acquaintance. The fact that the latter is familiar with the fate of both Heinrich and his father indicates that he is also the antiquary who had told the elder Ofterdingen of the blue flower as well as the stranger of the first chapter of the novel. Sylvester, we may gather from his conversations with Heinrich, was to instruct Heinrich in the natural sciences so that he, like the youth of the Atlantis fable, might combine in his person the spirits of both poetry and nature. Heinrich sees in Sylvester's flowering garden amongst the ruins a symbol of the life cycle of the world: "Your garden is the world. Ruins are the mothers of these flourishing children. The colorful, living creation draws its nourishment from the shattered remains of past ages. But did the mother have to die so that the children might prosper . . .?" (I, 231). His words recall the Communion-like image of the "Märchen," when the family drew new life from the body of the transfigured mother. The death and transfiguration of Mathilde have given Heinrich insight into the secrets of life.

The two men are led to a discussion of the phenomena of nature. Sylvester professes that an ethical force is the guiding principle of the universe. This force, he maintains, must be the guiding spirit of poetry too. It is the true spirit of religion and the thread which binds together the whole universe—doubtless the spiritual power symbolized in the "Märchen" by Sophie. Finally the conversation reveals that for Novalis poetry and science may be united in the same individual no matter which path he has first followed. "My concern for nature," Sylvester says, "has brought me to the point to which you were led by your delight in and enthusiasm for language" (I, 237). Poetry may bring the individual to a full appreciation of the rôle of the natural sciences or the opposite may be the case. The goals of both are the same in Novalis' eyes. Both seek to reveal the ethical force that is the guiding spirit of nature and to expose the great sympathy existing among all things. The ultimate function of both is to bring man back to the state of intimate communion with nature he had enjoyed in the Golden Age and to lead him on to knowledge of the transcendent.

Here the novel breaks off, but what awaited Heinrich is to considerable extent presaged in both the "Märchen" and in the first of his dreams, the dream of the blue flower. We recall that his dream followed upon the story of the flower told by a mysterious stranger and upon Heinrich's recollection of other stories of a Golden Age. The images of the dream itself pass at first in rapid sequence. Heinrich sees himself wandering through unknown lands, across seas and among strange animals and people. Scenes of war and turmoil are replaced by an image of quiet dwellings. Then he sees himself in prison and suffering great distress. He dies and is reborn, loves passionately and is separated from his beloved. Finally the images crystallize in one final scene. Heinrich finds himself climbing a rocky path after passing through a dark wood. Within a cave he finds a corridor leading to a large opening from which streams brilliant light. The source of this light is a golden ray which rises like a fountain to the roof of the cave, there to shatter into sparks that collect as liquid in a bowl below. The touch of this liquid is like spiritual inspiration. As Heinrich immerses himself in it, it seems to have procreative and erotic qualities: ". . . new pictures that he had never seen before took shape, these flowed together and became visible creatures all about him, and every wave of this lovely element pressed close to him like a delicate bosom. The waters seemed like a solution composed of bewitching girls taking shape the instant they touched him" (". . . neue, niegesehene Bilder entstanden, die auch ineinanderflossen und zu sichtbaren Wesen um ihn wurden, und jede Welle des lieblichen Elements schmiegte sich wie ein zarter Busen an ihn. Die Flut schien eine Auflösung reizender Mädchen, die an dem Jünglinge sich augenblicklich verkörperten" [1, 102f]). Intoxicated by this experience he swims along a stream which flows from the bowl into the rock, falling asleep and dreaming (within the dream) as he goes, only to be awakened by a light of a different quality. Whereas gold had dominated the cave, blue predominates in this new realm: "Dark blue rocks . . . the sky was blue-black and perfectly clear" ("Dunkelblaue Felsen . . . der Himmel war schwarz-blau und völlig rein" [I, 103]). His attention is captured, however, by a blue flower which changes shape as he is about to approach it. Just before he is awakened by his mother's voice, Heinrich sees a beautiful face among the flower's petals.

The first series of images in the dream, which suggest a long period of wandering and experiences of great variety, need no amplification. The final scene is more difficult of explanation, but its imagery lends itself to interpretation. The path leading through the dark wood and up the cliff to the cave suggests an arduous course that will eventually bring Heinrich to his goal. The penetration to the inner cave along the corridor hints at his penetration to the secrets of life. Gold, the traditional symbol of man's most precious possessions, dominates the inner cave and may well represent attainment to the highest earthly lot. His immersion in the liquid with its erotic qualities, there to fall asleep and dream as he swims along the stream, suggests the experience of death, the final dream. In the *Hymnen* we find the dream as a symbol of death, while eroticism is invariably associated with death in Novalis' other works. The same erotic imagery, too, is to be found in the song of the dead, incorporated into Tieck's account of the completed work ("Lobt doch unsre stillen Feste" [I, 252ff]). Evidence in Novalis' notes corroborates this interpretation: "The conclusion is the transition from the real to the secret world— death—final dream and awakening" ("Der Schluss ist Übergang aus der wirklichen Welt in die geheime—Tod—letzter Traum und Erwachen" [I, 241]). If this interpretation is correct, it is then death and a new life after death which brings Heinrich into the final realm of the dream, the realm of the flowers. At other points in Novalis' work we have seen flowers as symbols of spiritual values and an entry in Novalis' diary, made when he was at work on *Ofterdingen*, is a further clue to the nature of this flower realm: "There are so many flowers in this world that are of supernatural origin, flowers which do not prosper in this clime and which are actually heralds, messengers crying of a better existence. Among these flowers belong primarily religion and love" (IV, 403). The flower realm of the dream would then seem to be like the realm of Arcturus in the "Märchen." There, it will be recalled, were flowers, petrified at the beginning of the "long night," which burst into life in the new Golden Age. This is the heaven of Novalis, the spiritual realm where nature exists in ideal form, and where the final secrets of life were to be revealed to Heinrich as he found the blue flower.

The blue flower that has become the symbol of German Romanticism is certainly the most important image of *Heinrich von Ofterdingen*. It is kept in the forefront of the work, not only as it appears from time to time at important moments in the action, but also by the many occasions on which there is allusion to the color blue. (Sophie's veil is blue, a blue flame burns on the hearth of the hut in the Atlantis fable, Freya lies beneath a blue coverlet, the water from Sophie's altar turns into a blue vapor when it touches Ginnistan and the children, etc.) [1] We meet the flower itself on three occasions after the dream: as Heinrich is about to leave Thuringia; immediately before his encounter with the Saracen maiden; after his first meeting with Mathilde. To these may be added the vision of the flower in Klingsohr's "Märchen." That the blue flower has symbolic value is made clear first by allusion to it as "die blaue Blume," the definite article suggesting its uniqueness, and then by the fact that the flower appears in the dreams of both father and son. Its relationship to Mathilde and to the spirit of poetry is made plain subsequently in the work. Since the blue flower is the final image of Heinrich's dream, it would seem that the last act of the novel was to be the finding of its meaning. The fact that the blue flower is before Heinrich at three important moments in his development does not preclude its being the symbol of his final goal. It is rather that the vision of the goal draws him onward, keeping itself ever before him. The ultimate symbolic value of the blue flower cannot be definitely stated with the evidence available to us, though it is certain that the blue flower and Mathilde are one. As we have seen, Mathilde symbolizes both love and the spirit of poetry. There is evidence, too, that she represents a universal mother image, equated with

---

[1] *Cf.* "Paralipomena": "Everything blue in my book . . ." ("Alles blau in meinem Buche . . ." [I, 245]). Novalis may have been influenced by Goethe's theories of the qualities of colors. *Cf.* the characterization of blue in the "Farbenlehre": "Blue draws us to it" ("Das Blaue zieht uns nach sich") (Weimar Ausgabe, II, Abt. I, 314f). Possible sources for the blue flower are suggested by Jutta Hecker, *Das Symbol der blauen Blume im Zusammenhang mit der Blumensymbolik der Romantik,* Jenaer Germanistische Forschungen, XVII (Jena, 1931). Hecker points first to a Kyffhäuser legend of a flower that reveals hidden treasure to those who find it, then to Jean Paul's *Die unsichtbare Loge,* in which the hero, Gustav, sees a magic flower in a dream.

the Virgin, and is thus a symbol of the life principle itself, revealed through love and poetry. We recall that Hyazinth found beneath the veil of the goddess the Rosenblüte whose love had always been his. Perhaps a similar discovery awaited Heinrich. Perhaps in the blue flower he was to find the final knowledge of the love, poetic spirit, and secrets of life that had always been about him and within him in the person of Mathilde. The recurrent spiral image suggests to me that such was, indeed, to be the case.

The imagery of the "Astralis" poem indicates that the action of the second part was to parallel in some measure the action of Klingsohr's "Märchen." Several notes made by Novalis support this contention. Some of these, indeed, identify characters in the larger work with figures in the fable: "Heinrich's mother is Fantasy . . . Schwaning is the Moon and the antiquary is the miner . . . and also Iron . . . Emperor Friedrich is Arcturus" ("Heinrichs Mutter ist Phantasie . . . Schwaning ist der Mond und der Antiquar ist der Bergmann . . . und auch das Eisen . . . Kaiser Friedrich ist Arctur" [I, 241]). The symbolic nature of the characters in the fragment and the allusions to their relationships to one another points to their reappearance in different though recognizable form. Thus we have seen that Sylvester is the antiquary of the first chapter, and there are suggestions in the text itself that he is also the miner and the stranger who first told Heinrich of the blue flower. In Cyane we meet the dead daughter of Hohenzollern restored to life. We may assume, then, that Heinrich's wanderings were to bring him again face to face with those who had helped shape him, as is suggested by Hohenzollern's words when Heinrich took leave of him (even though Hohenzollern there refers specifically to a reunion in heaven). The recurrent image of the conflict between the spirit of poetry and the forces hostile to it, in the "Märchen" and elsewhere in the fragment, points to a broader depiction of this conflict in the second part. At some point in the action it would seem likely that Heinrich was to journey to the Holy Land. This assumption is rendered more probable by the many allusions to the East as the birthplace of poetry and by Heinrich's meeting with the Saracen maid. Here, perhaps, Heinrich's poetry was to have united Christian and non-Christian worlds even as Christian and pagan worlds are united in the "Märchen" through the transformation of Eros and the revitalization of ancient myth.[2] The spiral image points to his eventual return, after a period of purification and growth, to his point of origin,[3] there to discover the secret of the blue flower. Certain images link Mathilde with Freya of the "Märchen." Eros sees Freya in the calyx of the dream-flower even as Heinrich's first sight of Mathilde was of her face among the petals of the blue flower in his dream. Freya, from whose body flow the electrical impulses identified with life-giving power, is, like Mathilde, a symbol of the life principle. Thus it seems likely that Heinrich was to play essentially the rôles of both Fabel and Eros, with the end of the novel depicting a new Golden Age in a world ruled by the spirit of love, peace and poetry.[4]

Many themes not touched upon in this discussion are to be found in the notes and sketches made by Novalis, though it is impossible to say which of these were actually to be incorporated into the completed work. The author's own uncertainty is at times apparent. One theme to which there is more than one reference and which, I feel certain, was to have been included in the complete work is Heinrich's undergoing a series of metamorphoses and living as flower, animal, rock and star,[5] thus enabling him to experience directly the great sympathy of all things to which there is so often allusion in the fragment. The revelation of this great sympathy and the knowledge of it enjoyed by man in the original

[2] Cf. "Paralipomena": "Heinrich . . . comes to Jerusalem . . . Reconciliation of the Christian and pagan religions" ("Heinrich . . . kommt nach Jerusalem . . . Aussöhnung der christlichen Religion mit der heidnischen" [I, 246]).

[3] There is an image in the dream of Heinrich's father for which there is no corresponding image in the youth's: "After a long time I entered a large cave, where sat an old man before an iron table . . . His beard had grown through the iron table and covered his feet" ("Nach langer Zeit kam ich in eine grosse Höhle, da sass ein Greis . . . vor einem eisernen Tische . . . Sein Bart war durch den eisernen Tisch gewachsen und bedeckte seine Füsse" [I, 107]). The allusion is clearly to the Kyffhäuser legend of Barbarossa. The only explanation I can offer for the inclusion of this image is that it is further evidence that the secret of the blue flower is to be found in Thuringia, at Heinrich's point of origin.

[4] Cf. "Paralipomena": "It is the primeval world, the Golden Age, at the end" ("Es ist die Urwelt, die goldne Zeit am Ende" [I, 244]).

[5] Cf. "Paralipomena": "Heinrich von Afterdingen becomes flower, animal, stone, star" ("Heinrich von Afterdingen wird Blume, Tier, Stein— Stern" [I, 241]).

Golden Age was, it would seem, to have been the prime function of Heinrich's poetry.

In the opening paragraph of his account of the projected action of "Die Erfüllung" Ludwig Tieck remarks: "Not only for the author's friends but for art itself it is an irreparable loss that he was not able to finish this novel, the originality and great purpose of which would have been even more apparent in the second part than in the first" (I, 250). Unhappily true as Tieck's statement is, speculation as to what might have been is, in the end, fruitless. Despite the obvious limitations of a work only half-completed, *Heinrich von Ofterdingen* ranks nevertheless among the most significant productions of the German Romantics. None surpasses it in terms of its contribution to the development of a peculiarly Romantic mode of presentation. In both form and content, indeed, *Heinrich von Ofterdingen* is the Romantic novel *par excellence*. Even in its fragmentary form it remains an impressive monument both to Novalis' remarkable creative powers and to the Romantic belief in the power of poetry to reveal the transcendent through the immanent.

CHAPTER IX

CONCLUSIONS

The influence Novalis has exerted on succeeding generations of poets and the acclaim that has been his scarcely seem commensurate with the limited quantity of his poetry. Small as is the body of his work, it bears the stamp of decided originality. It is this individuality in both his themes and techniques that has given his poetry its lasting freshness. Novalis' development of an unconventional and personal mode of expression is the more remarkable when we recall the trite nature of most of his early verse. To be sure, there remain in his major works some conventional elements. Readily identifiable too are occasional faults of redundancy, exaggerated hyperbole, and digression that can equally be attributed to his relative immaturity as an artist. The emergence of Novalis' genius was comparatively sudden. He died before having reached full artistic maturity. His youthful faults are insignificant, however, when contrasted to the many positive qualities of his work. The imaginative nature of his themes, the lyric intensity of his language, his strikingly evocative metaphor, the rich color that permeates his poetry—these are but a few of the qualities which spring to mind when one thinks of Novalis. His efforts to explore the ultimate expressive powers of language have made his work a source of stimulation for later poets. Indubitably the foremost poetic talent of the Early Romantic school, Novalis ranks among the most inventive of German poets. Few individuals have contributed as much to the growth of a literary movement as has Novalis. That the movement is in this case Romanticism, the longest lived and most important movement in German literature, makes Novalis' contribution the more significant. Novalis gave to German Romanticism its first great creative impulse and provided a model of Romantic style for those who came after. It is fitting

that from his poetry should have come the symbol of that movement, the blue flower.

Important as Novalis is as a pioneer of Romantic poetic techniques, he is equally important in terms of his influence on the
choice of subject matter of his successors. There are few themes
in later Romantic literature that are not to be found in his work.
Indeed, Novalis might well be called the prototype of the German
Romantic poet. With him, too, begins that tendency for which
critics, following Goethe's example, have most often castigated
the German Romantics—the tendency to seek in Christianity the
answers to the problems of life and death. It has often been
claimed that underlying this tendency is an antagonism or a sense
of revulsion toward this world and its life. The hero of Thomas
Mann's *Tonio Kröger* tells his confidante: "People have said—
they have even written and published it—that I hate or fear life, or
despise or loathe it." The same words have, in effect, been used
of Novalis. Yet such a characterization is unjust, failing, as it does,
to take note of much that is expressed in his writings. Death, it is
true, occupies a place in the forefront of Novalis' works. Indeed,
virtually all his later works may be said to be concerned ultimately
with the problem of death. Yet equally prominent in these works—
and perhaps more important—is the poet's concern for the
knowledge of life that is gained from the understanding of death's
true meaning. Novalis' dream-vision, to which he alludes on
several occasions in his writings, brought him a revelation of the
relationship of life and death that transformed his existence. His
conviction that death is but a door to a richer, fuller life in eternity
persuaded him of the truths of the Christian doctrine. The poetic
works of his last years are the fruits of this experience. In them
Novalis seeks to show the meaning for mankind of his unique
revelation. It is not only the conviction that man may in heaven
attain to knowledge of the secrets of life that is the source of the
joy so evident in these works. For Novalis there is the further
promise that man may in this life have foretaste of the delights of
heaven. With the acceptance of Christ as Saviour comes full
understanding of life, an appreciation of its beauty and true value.
Through Christ (and therefore in the full renunciation of all
attempts to interpret life and death rationally), man may hope to
recapture the blissful state of naive innocence in intimate com-

munion with nature which, Novalis believes, mankind had once enjoyed. For through Him all can be understood, all can be meaningful and beauteous. Fear of the unknown, that fear which had destroyed the Golden Age of the childhood of man, disappears with the revelation of Christ's victory over death.

Two media other than religious inspiration itself, Novalis indicates, afford mankind direct knowledge of divine truth. Love and poetry, those flowers blooming in a foreign clime, are envoys on earth of the realm of the spirit. Love that has been purified by Christ binds together earth and heaven. Through its intoxicating and inspiring power the individual may grasp the mysteries of life and death. Poetry, the creation of a divinely inspired imagination, reveals knowledge to which rational thought cannot aspire. By its power to make known the transcendent through the immanent poetry can lead man to ultimate truth. Through poetry and love, then, the individual may on earth recapture for himself the lost Golden Age.

The nonrational beliefs to which Novalis clung became the central themes of his later works. To present the nondemonstrable truths he grasped intuitively and to make palpable the inexpressible, Novalis turned to poetry rather than to philosophic treatise. In the language of metaphor he found the one medium appropriate to his visionary utterances. His work has the character of a brilliantly colorful tapestry, the individual pictures of which are brought into relationship through a skillfully woven pattern of recurrent imagery. Because of the frequency with which certain metaphors are encountered, they may be regarded as elements of a fixed system of private symbols. Conventional and traditional as some of these are, the poet has made them his own through his preferred, perhaps instinctive, use of them to express ideas or attitudes he cherishes. We have observed their growth in his poetry and thus may state with reasonable certainty what these are and what is their value for the poet.

The image we meet most frequently in Novalis is, of course, that of a new Golden Age. This is, however, but one element of a threefold metaphorical representation of the growth of individual and mankind to full knowledge of the transcendent. To this broad image are related all the elements of the poet's private system of symbols. The first phase in man's history is depicted as an original

Golden Age, the childhood of man. It is characterized by man's apprehension of the spiritual through representation. In the portrayal of this phase, therefore, we find spiritual values personified in the gods of ancient myth, or the worship of supernatural forces represented in the sun and the stars. This first period is invariably seen as an age of blissful naïveté, faith and fantasy. It came to an end, it is suggested, because of man's fear of death, the horrifying riddle to which he could find no satisfactory answer. The failure of myth and secular religions to interpret adequately the problem of death, Novalis implies, robbed man of his childlike faith and happiness, bringing this idyllic state to a close. The middle period is characterized by the growth into adulthood. Then man puts irrational emotionalism behind him and seeks through rational thought to master the secrets of life and death. Novalis represents this phase most poignantly in an image of a desolate waste, chilled by freezing winds and devoid of blossoming growth. Man moves from an Eden to a polar region. It is an age of discord, strife and barbarism. While man gropes blindly in a darkened universe, spiritual values—the "benevolent goddesses"—battle with the forces hostile to them. The final phase sees man's attainment to knowledge of the divine. Spiritual values triumph and are restored to their rightful place as the guiding powers of the universe. A variety of metaphor embodies the nature of this new Golden Age. Invariably it is depicted as a new spring, a time of sudden blossoming and of life springing from graves and the lifeless earth. Always, too, we find allusion to the flowing together of heaven and earth, of spiritual and physical realms. Associated with it, explicitly or implicitly, is the revelation of the true nature of death by Christ. Thus to the pagan concept of a Golden Age is joined the Christian heaven as well as the notion of paradise regained. Then a new poetic spirit, inspired by the revelation of Christ, recreates the myth of life. Through the new myth there is revitalized the myth that had given the first age meaning and beauty even as the gods of the first phase are reborn in Christ. Here, as in the Golden Age of his childhood, man enjoys intimate communion with nature, conversing with plants, rocks and animals. As the individual recaptures his lost innocence, he discovers the hidden secrets of life and the world.

Light and color images intensify this depiction of growth to knowledge of the divine. Physical light, represented variously as the sun, the day, or as lamps, symbolizes secularism and rationalism. With this image of physical light is invariably associated the belief that death marks the end of man's existence. Thus the destruction of this belief is frequently represented as the death of the sun. (It is to this, I suggest, that a note in the "Paralipomena" to *Ofterdingen* has reference: "The blue flower is still governed by the seasons. Heinrich breaks this spell—destroys the sun's dominion" ("Die blaue Blume richtet sich noch nach den Jahreszeiten. Heinrich vernichtet diesen Zauber—zerstört das Sonnenreich" [I, 241]). One might expect that the antitheses of the powers represented by physical light would be portrayed as night or darkness. This is rarely the case. Instead, the power of the divine and the victory of life over death are seen as another form of light, greater than physical light. Only in the *Hymnen an die Nacht* does night have fixed symbolic value for Novalis. To this must be contrasted the "long night" of Klingsohr's "Märchen" and the images of night and darkness in the sacred songs, all of which represent, in effect, the middle phase of man's development. Even in the hymns to the night we find allusion to a "light of night's heaven" and to a "sun of night." Elsewhere we find metaphors of flame, sparks and fire that revitalize the lifeless middle period. Perhaps the most striking representation of this concept, however, is to be found in Klingsohr's fable in the rainbow-like source of new light which replaces that of the burned-out sun. Related to these last light images are those which portray the light emanating from precious stones. The quality of these images is to suggest subtly that such objects may reveal the sympathy existing between physical and spiritual realms. Similarly, color imagery reveals the presence or absence of spiritual values. The middle period is remarkable for its drabness, while the Golden Age, old and new, sparkles with brilliant colors. Specific symbolic value, of course, attaches to the color blue in *Ofterdingen,* where its presence invariably implies some manifestation of the divine.

Invariably joined with those images representing the attainment to the final state is bold erotic metaphor. Here again we may speak of fixed symbolic value, for eroticism is always identified with apprehension of the spiritual. Most frequently this imagery depicts the power of love to transform and to reveal. Thus, through such metaphor, Novalis identifies eroticism with the love of Christ as a mode of communication with the divine. It must be emphasized that at no point is erotic imagery subordinated to the Christian. The two are daringly juxtaposed. Death itself is experienced as erotic passion, while eternity is seen in images of an everlasting nuptial night. The dawn of eternity is heralded in Klingsohr's fable by the transformation of the throne into a bridal bed, as lover embraces beloved. From Novalis' early poetry to his last works water images are representative of eroticism. Water is identified explicitly by the intensely emotional youth in *Die Lehrlinge zu Sais* as the erotic element. Elsewhere we find thirst and sexual appetite equated. Like the explicitly erotic metaphors cited above, water imagery then depicts death and transfiguration, with the final *unio mystica* a vaporous commingling in the "Hymns to Night." Eroticism is, then, implicit in the frequently met image of the flowing together of physical and spiritual realms. A similar value attaches to an equally constant image, that of twilight. Implicit in this representation is the flowing together of immanent and transcendent as physical light ends and the greater light of night approaches.

Two distinct values are found for the dream image in Novalis' poetry. On occasion we meet the "oppressive" dream or dream of pain, its nature always made known through epithet. In this case the dream graphically characterizes the "unreal" existence of the middle period. Otherwise the dream image symbolizes the rich, full life of the eternal Golden Age, whether in direct experience of it or as anticipatory enjoyment. Music images have established connotation after they are first met in *Die Lehrlinge zu Sais*. These represent the creative forces and ordered pattern of nature and the universe. Dissonance, as might be expected, then suggests man in his middle phase clumsily seeking to reproduce this harmony. Finding expression in music images too is the sympathetic bond between man and nature, while the relationship of the artist to the creative forces of the universe is suggested by his power to compose song. The image of the stringed instrument as a symbol of the poet's vocation and genius grows almost naturally from the original music images depicting nature's creative forces.

Certain metaphors of animistic projection develop unchanging values. Stones, stars, trees, and animals are invariably endowed

with human attributes or spiritual qualities. Through these metaphors, particularly, Novalis reveals one of his most cherished
beliefs—that all things exist in one another and that all are united
by an indefinable bond. For Novalis, nature is understandable
only as a living creature with emotional attributes analogous to
those of man. (Thus he regards the farmer and the miner as
curators of spiritual values equally with the artist and the musician.) It is somewhat surprising that in the poetry of the creator
of the blue flower we meet few metaphors of animistic projection
in the form of flower images. When these occur, however, they
invariably symbolize the spiritual life attained to by man in his
final phase as well as the gentle spirit, beauty and richness of
that life.

Although the blue flower is the best known of Novalis' symbols,
two other images are of ultimately greater significance for the
understanding of his work. The images of the spiral and the veil
recur as fixed symbols in the poetry of his last years. These are,
I believe, the most important individual symbols in Novalis, for
in them he has embodied his view of man's existence. The spiral
image grows directly from the constant depiction of man's progress
as the following of a path. The figure man describes on his road
toward ultimate truth is that of a spiral, for he returns eventually
to his point of origin but at a higher level. Through his efforts to
recapture the lost Golden Age the individual attains to a state of
conscious naïveté, a state fuller and richer than his original state
of innocent naïveté. It is a requisite for the attainment to the final
stage of communion with the divine. The idea of such a course
of development is inherent in the concept of the Golden Age
regained—a state both old and new, familiar and yet strange, the
same and yet more than the original state. Into this figure of a
spiral is compressed the course of action of both Novalis' novels,
while in his recurrent metaphor of "going home" the concept is
given poignantly simple expression. The veil image is invariably
present, explicitly or implicitly, in Novalis' depiction of the middle
phase, for then nature, truth, and spiritual values are always
hidden from man by a veil of his own making. The image represents both the false culture that has divorced man from nature
and the rational thought processes which constantly frustrate his
efforts to recapture his lost happiness. Beneath the veil, obscured

and yet occasionally glimpsed in moments of inspiration, are the beauty, mystery and wonder of the life that might be ours.

Novalis found in poetic imagery the special language within language to which reference was made at the beginning of this study. It became for him a mode of communication with those he called the "initiated," those sympathetic to poetry and to himself. Through metaphor he has succeeded in creating a private language by which to impart his convictions to those responsive to figurative representation. His belief in the metaphorical nature of life and the world about him finds appropriate expression in his work in the metaphorical representation of all that concerns him. His imagery is often bold and esoteric; always it has a highly imaginative quality. Through such metaphor he is able to burst the bonds of conventional language. His work, as a result, presents a challenge to the imagination of the reader. For those unresponsive to figurative language Novalis' poetry must remain a riddle. The veil of imagery he has cast over his poetry hides from those he called "the profane" his convictions, his faith and the truths he grasped intuitively. For those, however, who share Novalis' love of figurative representation and his belief in the power of metaphor to reveal hidden truths it is a veil that enhances, rather than conceals, the beauty of his art.

BIBLIOGRAPHY

I. EDITIONS OF NOVALIS' WORKS

Schriften, ed. Ernst Heilborn, 3 vols. (Berlin, 1901).
Schriften, ed. Jacob Minor, 4 vols. (Jena, 1907).
Schriften, eds. Paul Kluckhohn and Richard Samuel, 4 vols. (Leipzig, 1929).
Werke und Briefe, ed. Ewald Wasmuth, 5 vols. (Heidelberg, 1943-1955).
Gesammelte Werke, ed. Carl Seelig, 5 vols. (Zürich, 1945-1946).

II. CRITICAL STUDIES IN ENGLISH OF NOVALIS' WORKS

Hiebel, Friedrich. *Novalis. German Poet—European Thinker—Christian Mystic*, University of North Carolina Studies in the Germanic Languages and Literatures, X (Chapel Hill, 1954).
Peacock, Ronald. "Novalis and Schopenhauer: a Critical Transition in Romanticism," *German Studies Presented to L. A. Willoughby* (Oxford, 1952), pp. 133-143.
Peacock, Ronald. "The Poetry of Novalis," *German Studies Presented to H. G. Fiedler* (Oxford, 1938), pp. 323-344.
Spring, Powell. *Novalis. Pioneer of the Spirit* (Winterpark, Florida, 1946).

III. A SELECTION OF CRITICAL STUDIES IN GERMAN OF NOVALIS' WORKS

Albrecht, Luitgart. *Der magische Idealismus in Novalis' Märchentheorie und Märchendichtung* (Hamburg, 1948).
Beheim-Schwarzbach, Martin. *Novalis* (Stuttgart, 1948).
Biser, E. *Abstieg und Auferstehung. Die geistige Welt in Novalis' Hymnen an die Nacht* (Heidelberg, 1954).
Carlsson, Annie. *Die Fragmente des Novalis* (Basel, 1939).
Diez, Max. "Metapher und Märchengestalt: III. Novalis und das allegorische Märchen," *PMLA*, XLVIII (June 1933), 488-507.
Fauteck, H. *Die Sprachtheorie des Novalis* (Berlin, 1940).
Feilchenfeld, Walter. *Der Einfluss Jacob Böhmes auf Novalis* (Berlin, 1920).
Goldammer, Kurt. *Novalis und die Welt des Ostens* (Stuttgart, 1948).
Hederer, Edgar. *Novalis* (Vienna, 1949).
Heilborn, Ernst. *Novalis der Romantiker* (Berlin, 1901).
Hiebel, Friedrich. *Novalis. Der Dichter der blauen Blume* (Bern, 1951).
Jaeger, Hans Peter. *Hölderlin—Novalis. Grenzen der Sprache* (Zürich, 1949).
Kamla, Henry. *Novalis' Hymnen an die Nacht* (Copenhagen, 1945).
Kohlschmidt, Werner. "Der Wortschatz der Innerlichkeit bei Novalis," *Form und Innerlichkeit. Beiträge zur Geschichte und Wirkung der deutschen Klassik und Romantik*, Sammlung Dalp, No. 81 (Bern, 1955), pp. 120-156.

Kommerell, Max. "Novalis: Hymnen an die Nacht," *Gedicht und Gedanke,* ed. H. O. Burger (Halle, 1942), pp. 202-236.

Müller-Seidel, Walter. "Probleme neuerer Novalis-Forschung," *Germanisch-Romanische Monatschrift,* Neue Folge III, H.4 (October 1953), 274-292.

Obenauer, Karl Justus. *Hölderlin—Novalis* (Jena, 1925).

Ritter, Heinz. *Novalis' Hymnen an die Nacht* (diss. Heidelberg, 1930).

Samuel, Richard. *Die poetische Staats- und Geschichtsauffassung Friedrich von Hardenbergs,* Deutsche Forschungen, XII (Frankfurt am Main, 1925).

Schneider, Reinhold. *Der Dichter vor der Geschichte. Hölderlin—Novalis* (Heidelberg, 1946).

Ziegler, Klaus. "Die Religiosität des Novalis im Spiegel der 'Hymnen an die Nacht'," *Zeitschrift für deutsche Philologie,* LXX (1947-1949), 396-417, LXXI (1953), 256-277.

IV. GENERAL WORKS

Babbitt, Irving. *Rousseau and Romanticism* (Boston and New York, 1919).

Clemen, Wolfgang. *The Development of Shakespeare's Imagery* (Cambridge, Mass., 1949).

Curtius, Ernst Robert. *Europäische Literatur und Lateinisches Mittelalter* (Bern, 1948).

Dilthey, Wilhelm. *Das Erlebnis und die Dichtung,* 6th ed. (Leipzig and Berlin, 1919).

Gode-von Aesch, Alexander. *Natural Science in German Romanticism* (New York, 1941).

Gray, Ronald D. *Goethe the Alchemist* (Cambridge, 1952).

Hewett-Thayer, Harvey W. *Hoffmann. Author of "The Tales"* (Princeton, 1948).

Kluckhohn, Paul. *Die deutsche Romantik* (Bielefeld and Leipzig, 1924).

Lewis, C. Day. *The Poetic Image* (London, 1947).

Mustard, Helen M. *The Lyric Cycle in German Literature* (New York, 1946).

Rehm, Walther. *Orpheus. Der Dichter und die Toten. Selbstdeutung und Totenkult bei Novalis—Hölderlin—Rilke* (Düsseldorf, 1950).

Silz, Walter. *Early German Romanticism. Its Founders and Heinrich von Kleist* (Cambridge, Mass., 1929).

Strich, Fritz. *Deutsche Klassik und Romantik,* 4th ed. (Bern, 1949).

INDEX